Where the Hawthorn Grows

An American Druid's Reflections

Morgan Daimler

MOON BOOKS

Winchester, UK
Washington, USA

First published by Moon Books, 2013
Moon Books is an imprint of John Hunt Publishing Ltd., Laurel House, Station Approach,
Alresford, Hants, SO24 9JH, UK
office1@jhpbooks.net
www.johnhuntpublishing.com
www.moon-books.net

For distributor details and how to order please visit the 'Ordering' section on our website.

ISBN: 978 1 78099 969 2

A CIP catalogue record for this book is available from the British Library.

Design: Stuart Davies

Printed and bound by CPI Group (UK) Ltd, Croydon, CR0 4YY

CONTENTS

This book is dedicated to all who seek Truth and walk the Druid's path.

With thanks to my family; Scott, Amara, Paige and Terry who have always supported my dreams and put up with the time I spend writing.

And my friends, especially Allison, Tricia, Mel, Steph, Donnalee, Eilidh, Moonwriter, Saille, Maya, Blackbird, and all the Druids of the OWO and Grove of Two Coasts.

Introduction

This book represents my own personal experiences and thoughts about Irish-based reconstructionist Druidism. These opinions and experiences are shaped by the fact that I am part of the Irish Diaspora, living not in Ireland but in America. I do not see this as a weakness in any way but as a unique challenge to find ways to adapt and connect to the land I live on in a Celtic way; the Celts themselves, after all, were people who migrated and traveled, settling in new lands which they made their own.

Being a Druid is a part of who I am, and it is a title I have worked hard to earn over the course of many years. Modern Druidism is an extremely diverse religion, with many different expressions and approaches, but one of the most unique of those is based on reconstructionism. This approach is gaining in popularity as more and more people are seeking out the threads of history to weave the future of this spiritual path.

My own spirituality is complex and in this book I have tried to present it as it is, because I know that I am not the only one who struggles to find balance between different cultures. My primary focus is Irish, but I also have some Norse and continental Celtic influences that affect how I do things and what I believe. I hope that seeing how one person approaches these things may help others.

My writing is also influenced by other aspects of my life including my family, my children, and my involvement in the larger pagan community in my area. My spirituality is an integral part of my life and so being a Druid cannot be separated out from being a wife, mother, friend, or teacher, and vice versa. In the same way, my preference for a reconstructionist approach to religion and magic invariably influences how I look at things and what I believe.

What follows are my thoughts, opinions, beliefs, and

practices, shaped over decades of practice. I hope this book can be of use to others and that through sharing my own ideas other people will be inspired on their own paths.

Chapter 1

Beliefs and Practices

Why Reconstruction?

The question is asked, sooner or later, when people find out that a person follows a reconstructionist approach, why reconstruction? While I no longer think of myself as a Celtic reconstructionist (or CR) per se, I do feel that reconstruction is a big part of my own practice and I enjoyed thinking about the question. Reconstructionism is an approach which uses historical evidence, mythology, folklore, and secondary sources to understand what the original pagan faith would have been like. This is then used to envision what that kind of paganism might have been like if it had never ceased to be practiced.

I began in mainstream neopaganism but even at a young age was drawn to Irish material. Back in the early 1990s the only way to follow that up available to me was to delve into historic and mythic literature. This gave me at least a basic understanding of what was known about the actual beliefs and practices of the pagan Irish. Why I was drawn to the Irish is a bit of a separate topic, but suffice to say it was a longstanding interest nurtured by family heritage and stories. Later, when I began to find books by popular pagan authors that claimed to be genuine or traditionally Irish or Celtic, I was disappointed to see a decided lack of genuine material. I could never be satisfied following made-up or imagined Irish paganism. I think that quest for Truth is what led me into Druidism and I was lucky enough in the late 1990s to find a reconstructionist Druid discussion group (which later became an Order) and that gave me the concept of practicing modern paganism based on reconstructionist principles as a viable method. I say lucky because this was still a time when the majority of Druidic groups were solidly revivalist or neopagan; neither of which is bad, necessarily, but both of which include the very romanticism or outside influences I was trying to avoid. Finding the Order of the White Oak showed me not only that I wasn't alone in seeking to learn about the actual pagan practices but also that it was possible to shape those historic practices into something modern and fulfilling. In my own way I had been practicing reconstructionism without knowing what it was for several years, but finding other people was inspirational.

In the same way, though, I have an inherent need for mysticism and magic that pulled me beyond simply studying the material or keeping to the surface of practicing it. I was drawn to seek the practical applications of the most esoteric aspects of Irish paganism and to learn the magics talked about in the myths and stories that I read. In the end I think what drew me into Druidism was the desire to embody that same pagan magic I was reading about; at 14 I didn't want to be like the Driud Fedelm of the Ulster Cycle, I wanted to *be* Fedelm. Of course I was also driven from early on to serve my community as what can only be described as clergy. There is a certain inevitability in a person who is so driven by Irish culture, myth, and magic, and a call to serve, ending up being drawn to Druidism. Nonetheless I was never satisfied with the modern Druid groups who all either lacked something I was looking for or included something I was trying not to include myself. Only in finding a reconstructionist Druid Order did I find something that seemed to be exactly what I needed.

Being a reconstructionist satisfies my need for a solid historical basis while being a Druid satisfies my need for mysticism and magic. It probably seems like utter cognitive dissonance to some, but it is the only thing that really works for me, and that is why I am a reconstructionist and that is why I am a Druid as well.

The 'D' Word

Nothing is more useful in paganism or can cause more confusion than labels, and both of those apply in equal measure to the word 'Druid'. Labels, of course, serve an important purpose in connecting to people's schema and helping to give an instant understanding of what you're talking about or trying to convey; they create a common ground, although sometimes definitions differ and discussion is required to get on the same page.

The best words to describe my spirituality are probably págánacht and heathen, since the first is specific to Irish paganism and the second is general for an eclectic Norse/Germanic spirituality. I don't mix the two together, but rather follow them both separately; four holidays for one, four for the other and I am dedicated to a deity in each pantheon. Maybe this is not the ideal solution in some people's eyes, but it works for me. I like having nice single words to use as descriptors in a conversation because sometimes precision is a virtue. When I'm asked what my religion is or what path I follow and my answer is a paragraph-long explanation it tends to put people off, but a nice simple answer can open up further conversation and a more detailed follow up explanation. So instead of starting off with 'I'm an Irish reconstructionist and heathen who practices witchcraft', I generally tell people I am a Druid.

Druid is a highly controversial term in CR (Celtic reconstructionism) because many people feel the old Druids are dead and gone beyond being brought back. They were the educated class of their society, the doctors, lawyers, advisors, priests, seers, and elite musicians, so there is some weight to the argument that recreating them as they were is impossible. In modern usage the word has come to denote a practitioner of a religion, Druidism, although I personally don't see it as describing a religion but as a title for a position within a religion, like priestess or imam. That's what it was always supposed to mean, and it was only after the Druids were separated from Celtic paganism during the revival period in the 18th century (to allow Christians to be 'Druids') that it took on an -ism of its own; or a -ry depending on your viewpoint. I think those of us trying to reconstruct Celtic paganism should include the clergy (not everyone agrees with me) and go back more to the old model of Druids and lay people all practicing Celtic polytheism, but it may be that too much time has passed with Druidism being its own religion for that to ever happen. Things change and evolve.

So, having said that, why do I use the word Druid? Why call myself a Druid when I practice Irish paganism from a reconstructionist perspective and I know how controversial the word is? It would certainly be easier in some contexts not to call myself a Druid. Part of the answer is that I feel it is the best word I know to describe what I do in a public setting, as someone who acts as clergy to a larger community. Part of the answer is that I belong to a Druid Order and have earned the title through that Order. And it is the single word that best encompasses what I do and believe, even with the misconceptions and vagueness around the term, to use when talking to someone who is not a reconstructionist. Realistically, most of the people I talk to about religion have no idea what reconstructionism is, but everyone has some idea of what a Druid is. It gives me something to work with, a place to start and build on. So I use it because it does describe who I am and what I do and because it is an effective way to talk about my spirituality. Controversy and all.

Living Reconstruction

I've been talking lately with a couple friends about reconstructionism and, in the course of the conversation, we end up sharing stories of past experiences. Somehow the conversation had turned to the way that people often misunderstand what reconstruction is and the funny and frustrating discussions that result. That got me thinking about how many people really don't understand what reconstruction is all about. So the following is my attempt to clarify a couple things and my own impression of what reconstructionist religions are.

First off, many people seem to think that being a reconstructionist means trying to live like, or have the spirituality of, an ancient culture – sorry, no. Reconstruction is about learning as much as we can about what the ancient culture was like and what the religion was like in order to bring the core of it forward in a workable modern way. We are not trying to bring ourselves back or create a backwards looking religion, rather we want to envision what that ancient paganism would have grown into had it not been interrupted. By researching and using archaeology, anthropology, history, mythology, and linguistics we can gain a better understanding of the beliefs and practices that existed thousands of years ago and find the best ways to bring that forward in a viable modern way.

Secondly, reconstructionism is not a static faith; it is not only about picking out bits and pieces of old pagan practices to use. Achieving a thorough grounding in the ancient culture and the principles of modern reconstruction allows people to then create new material in the spirit of the old material; songs, poems, invocations, rituals, and all the other essentials. No religion can survive long if it is not living and growing and that is equally true of reconstructionism. Now it is true that new material has to be in line with the old, because part of reconstruction is not introducing foreign elements, but the world we live in today is very different from the world thousands of years ago – if we can't create a religion that is modern and that is adapted for the modern world, then really, what's the point?

So to me reconstruction is a viable modern faith that is rooted in an ancient pagan faith, brought forward as we envision it if it had never stopped being practiced. Each individual and every group will have their own ideas on what that would look like depending on their own views and interpretations of the available material, creating a very similar situation to what it was like back then, when each tribe had its own particular way within the larger culture. Nonetheless we all share a common goal and a common vision that should hold us together as a community. We keep the core cultural values, the main religious practices and beliefs, and we use critical thinking and inspiration, along with a deep understanding of the historical culture, to adapt the surviving material and to create new material in the spirit of the old. Reconstruction is not just about the book-knowledge or the research – it's about actively living the spirituality we find there.

Who Were the Druids?

Recently a friend asked a question – who were the Druids to the Celtic peoples? It's an interesting question and it made me think about exactly what role the Druids played within their society. The first hurdle is to decide where to start in looking for clues about who the Druids were. Every possible source of information has its flaws, either through the bias of the authors of secondary sources, or the bias of people interpreting harder evidence such as archeology. However, these flaws are not insurmountable and do not require that all evidence should be thrown out, especially when evidence from different sources is supportive of the same point. I think in the end we are left with secondary sources (Greek, Roman, and Christian) and mythology as well as supposition from archeology and anthropology to form a picture of who the Druids were. Each one offers a little piece of evidence and requires a certain cynicism.

Personally I have always rejected the common modern division of the Druids into 'bards, ovates, and druids', although I can see how this is a convenient way to divide up segments of study. As Dáithí O hÓgain says in his book The Sacred Isle:

> *Given their similarity in function abroad, and their interchangeability in Ireland, it seems best to regard these three terms druis, velitos, and vatis [druid, bard, and seer] as indicating the functions*

of the wise man among the ancient Celts. In the world of antiquity, we should not look for a clear distinction between great wisdom in its practical and sacred senses.
(O hÓgain, 1999).

So instead of seeing the Druids as divided into rigidly different segments, I think it more likely there was cross training that would have made each Druid able in the basics of each area, but allowed individuals to specialize.

I also don't agree with the idea some people put forth that an individual Druid was an expert in all things associated with Druidism. I think that the Druids filled a certain role within society as the educated class, if you will, and religious leaders, but that just like in today's professional careers there was specialization. A fair analogy for my view may be of someone in a modern setting who goes through a degree program and attends all the same basic classes, but also goes to classes in focused electives. So this is why, I think, we see Druids referred to as seers, priests, judges, advisors to kings, healers, and astronomers.

So, who do I think the Druids were?

To start, I think the Druids were concerned with any and all religious matters, both of doctrine and practice – Caesar tells us that 'Druids are concerned with religious matters, private and public sacrifice, and divination.' (Freeman, 2002). Diodorus also mentions the role of Druids:

The Gauls have certain wise men and experts on the Gods called druids, as well as a highly respected class of seers... It is a custom among the Gauls to never perform a sacrifice without someone skilled in divine ways present. They say that those who know about the nature of the Gods should offer thanks to them and make requests to them, as though these people spoke the same language as the Gods. The Gauls... obey the rule of the priests and bards...
(Freeman, 2002).

From this I gather that public religious ceremony required a Druid to preside. Caesar also mentions that a person brought before the Druids for judgment who ignored the ruling would be banned by the Druids from attending public ceremonies, and that this was viewed as an 'extremely harsh punishment' by the Gauls (Freeman, 2002). This reinforces the idea of the pivotal role that the Druids played within the society and in religious life.

I think the Druids were judges. Caesar, in his Gallic Wars, says, '...the Druids are the judges on all controversies public and private.' Strabo also comments in a similar way, saying, 'The Gauls consider the Druids the most just of people and so are entrusted with judging both public and private disputes.' (Freeman, 2002). I know it's common today to refer to them as lawyers, but I don't feel that's accurate because the modern idea of a lawyer carries associations that are simply not what the Druids actually did. In a modern context the word lawyer refers to people who advocate for a particular person or side in a dispute, and historically the Druids, as 'Brehon', did not do this but acted as judges or speakers of the law. The word in Irish 'breitheamh' (Old Irish brithem, plural brithemain) means judge, not lawyer. It's an issue of semantics in English but using the word lawyer implies action as an advocate, whereas judging is what they actually did. In the Old Law texts the Brehon (brithemain) always act as judges. The law texts do have a classification for a person who fills the role of an advocate, but that would be 'aigne' (that's the Old Irish). Fergus Kelly also discusses, in his book Early Irish Law, that people were often represented before the king or brithem by a fethem, a non-professional lawyer who was usually the head of the person's kin group (Kelly, 1988).

I think the Druids were seers. Although many references seem to separate the seers into a different category, it is also clear that the boundaries were fluid and that Druids were also seers; so I think, rather than three rigid categories, the Druids themselves were experienced as ritual leaders, seers, and bards. For example, in all the following cases the words 'Druid' and 'seer' are used interchangeably or a person identified as one is given the attributes/skills of the other:

> *The practice of divination is not even neglected by barbarians. I know there are Druids in Gaul because I met one myself... He would predict the future using augury and other forms of interpretation.*
> Cicero (Freeman, 2002).

> *Tiberius passed a decree through the senate outlawing their Druids and these types of diviners and physicians.*
> Pliny (Freeman, 2002).

> *The Druidess exclaimed to him as he went, 'Go ahead, but don't hope for victory or put any trust in your soldiers.'*
> Lamoridius on the emperor Alexander Severus receiving a prophecy when passing by a Druidess (Freeman, 2002).

Another account by Vopiscus relates a similar tale of Diocletian being told he would one day be emperor by a Druidess offering a spontaneous prophecy, and later the same writer says: 'On certain occasions Aurelian would consult Gaulish Druidesses to discover whether or not his descendants would continue to rule.' (Freeman, 2002).

Indeed, in The Sacred Isle by O hÓgain, the author points out that, 'Prophecy and divination are the accomplishments most frequently attributed to Druids in Irish literature,' which clearly establishes that there is no way to separate the concepts of seers and Druids from each other, particularly in the Irish (O hÓgain, 1999).

So we've looked at evidence supporting the roles of the Druids as ritual leaders, judges, and seers, but this is only a small piece of who the Druids were. We also have evidence that within their societies they were sacred poets, teachers of wisdom, the ones who understood the deeper mysteries of the natural world, and magic users. However, discussing the bardic role of Druids alone is fairly complicated.

The role of sacred poets, often called 'bards', is one of the most often written about topics, but at first glance it can give the appearance that the bards were a separate class from the Druids, especially in the continental material. In several of the Greek and Roman sources it is said that there were three types of men held in esteem, the bards, Druids, and seers, such as Strabo saying, 'Generally speaking, there are three uniquely honored groups among the Gauls: bards, vates, and Druids.' (Freeman, 2002). Adding to the confusion about the bards are several references that seem to place them in what we might see as a very low social position. Some examples of this:

> *They have singing poets called bards who perform playing an instrument like a Greek lyre. These bards sing songs of praise and of satire.*
> Diodorus Siculus (Freeman, 2002).

> *Posidonius of Apameia says... the Celts have with them in war and peace companions... [who] recite the praises of their patrons before gatherings and to all listening in turn. They are called bards – poets who sing praise.*
> Athenaeus (Freeman, 2002).

> *And the bards sang the great deeds of famous men in heroic verse, accompanied by the sweet tones of the lyre.*
> Ammianus Marcellinus (all – Freeman, 2002).

However, I think much like the false separation of the seers from the Druids discussed previously, the bards were in fact Druids. If we look at the Irish material it is much more apparent that this was the case as we see the same interchangeability of the terms that we saw in the continental use of Druid and vate. As O hÓgain explains it in The Sacred Isle:

> *In Irish they are all well attested as bard (a term for a minor poet or reciter), faidh (a prophet), and drui (a Druid or magician). All three words are to a large extent interchangeable, although bard is not generally accorded equal status with the others. Instead the Irish sources have fili (later, file) as a member of the exalted triad, and it is most plausible to regard this as having been the situation among the Continental Celts also.*
> (O hÓgain, 1999).

This may also explain why when reading material in translation we can sometimes find discrepancies, such as in different versions of the Tain Bo Cuilange where Fedelm is alternately called a prophetess, bard, or fairy.

I personally suspect that the account of continental bards who served in the retinue of 'patrons' represent Druidic bards of lower rank. The later Irish material also supports that possibility, although it is only speculation, as the Uraicecht Na Riar discusses the different grades of poets and, as with all things, it is likely that the majority of people remained in the lower ranks with only a few achieving the highest levels. This would mean many bards and fewer Fili.

It is also worth noting that while contemporary groups often emphasize the bard's role as poet or musician, in the ancient texts bards – or more accurately Fili – were equally skilled with magic, prophecy, and judgment, once again supporting the interchangeability of the role with that of the Druid. In the Cath Maige Tuired the File Coirpre laid a satire on the Fomorian King Bres who was ruling over the Tuatha Dé Danann for his lack of hospitality.

'Without food on a dish,
Without cow's milk on which a calf grows,
Without a man's habitation after darkness remains,
Without paying a company of storytellers – let that be Bres's condition,
Bres's prosperity no longer exists,' he said, and that was true.
There was only blight on him from that hour.
(Gray, 1983)

This demonstrates the poet's ability to magically curse with his art just as he could bless. In a similar way when the forces draw together for battle in the Cath Maige Tuired and Coirpre is asked what he will contribute to the fight he responds by pledging to make a satire against the Fomorian army that will weaken their warriors so that they offer no resistance (Gray, 1983).

The bard's skill with prophecy, something we have already seen is a Druidic art, is very often attested in the Irish material. In fact all of our surviving understanding of Druidic prophecy techniques – the dichetal do chennaibh, teinm laeda, and imbas forosnai – are attributed to 'poets', although we know that these were Druidic practices. Two of the three were outlawed in Ireland by the Church because they involved calling on pagan spirits or Gods. Interestingly the practice of bardcraft, or sacred poetry, survived well into the Christian era, nearly to the modern era, carrying with it many of the older practices associated with Druidic prophecy. For example, from A Description of the Western Isles of Scotland circa 1695:

I must not omit to relate their way of study, which is very singular: They shut their doors and windows for a day's time, and lie on their backs, with a stone upon their belly, and plaids about their heads, and their eyes being covered, they pump their brains for rhetorical encomium or panegyric; and indeed they furnish such a style from this dark cell, as is understood by very few; and if they purchase a

> *couple of horses as the reward of their meditation, they think they have done a great matter.*
> (Martin, 1695)

This is strikingly similar to the practice involved in the imbas forosnai, omitting only the initial eating of meat and adding the stone, but the elements of the practice seem to be related.

It is also worth noting that bards had a role as judges and that also connects them to the Druids. Both were able to make judgments against kings and assess a fine, or in the case of bards, possibly lay a satire. As O hÓgain puts it:

> *The functions of drui, file and faidh seem to have been interchangeable in archaic Irish with that for a judge (written brithem, later breitheamh) and... we can be sure that arbitration was also one of the functions of these wise men in Ireland.*
> (O hÓgain, 1999).

> *Should a poet, Druid, or Brithem make an unjust ruling their face would break out in blotches, a literal mark of shame.*
> (O hÓgain).

As we can see it is virtually impossible to truly separate out the different functions of the Druids into completely different groups. Each subgroup overlaps with the others and often the term used to describe a person would vary based entirely upon circumstance so that she might be called a Druidess and then a prophetess or bard in the next line of the same source. Of all of the subgroups the bards, or Fili, did seem to have the clearest distinctions in many cases, yet they still had the same blurring of function and interchangeability of labeling as any of the other groups that fall under the auspices of being a Druid.

References:

Kelly, F., (1988). Early Irish Law Freeman, P., (2002). War, Women, and Druids Gray, E., (1983) Cath Maige Tuired

O hÓgain, D., (1999). The Sacred Isle

Martin, M., (1695). A Description of the Western Isles

Living Honor

What does it mean to live an honorable life? Many modern pagan groups have outlined a list of basic virtues to nurture, and honor is usually included in each of them, but what is it to live honorably? How can we know how to shape our actions to live honorably when honor is often a difficult and obscure concept to define? The best approach, I think is not to look at honor as a single concept but rather to view it as a series of inter-related actions – because honor is an active principle not a passive idea – and look at how those actions combine to form a larger concept of honor. For those following an Irish path or looking to Irish myth for inspiration and guidance there is an abundance of suggestions on living with honor to be found.

There are several Irish texts that offer instructions on how a king should live in order to be a good king, and these texts serve as good instructions for anyone to study on how to live a good honorable life. One of the best of these is the Instruction of King Cormaic Mac Airt, a dialogue that occurs between Cairbre and Cormac, where Cairbre is quizzing Cormac about the proper qualities of a king. The answers given describe the characteristics a king should embody, but these characteristics are equally applicable to any person seeking to live a good life. These characteristics can be divided into two categories: ways that the person should act towards others, and ways that the person should uphold himself.

The dialogue response begins with Cormac describing ways that the king should act in order to uphold his own honor. The first of these is by having good geasa, or ritual taboos that are positive. This could apply to anyone who has a geas on them, if only in the way we choose to look at the ritual taboos that bind us. We can choose to see our taboos as positive or negative. How we react to them shapes their nature on some level, making them either a gift or a burden. The next line advises the king to be sober; good advice since drunkenness is often a source of trouble. The king is advised to be an invader as well, which is a slightly more obscure line. However, I believe that this advice pertains to ambition and the need for any person to have a healthy sense of what they can achieve. Only by pushing outward and seeking to expand can we truly achieve our own potential. The following lines suggest a good king should have good desires and be affable; telling us that people should seek to want what is best for themselves and have a friendly nature. A good king should be both humble and proud, meaning that we should be humble in knowing our own limits and admitting to our own mistakes, but also proud of what we do achieve and owning our own success; only through a balance of these two can true success be found. In the same way we should be quick and steadfast, meaning we should act quickly when speed is needed, but also have the stamina to stick with anything and see it through. A good king, or a good Druid, should be a poet, versed in legal lore, and wise, as well as temperate. All of these qualities should be embodied in the king for them to find the inner strength to live honorably in all these ways, because these external expressions reflect the character within, but they are equally applicable to anyone else seeking the same thing.

Cormac also touches on ways that a good king should interact with others, beginning with being generous, decorous, and sociable. These three features all intertwine to support each other and to support the proper social order where the king sets the tone for the kingdom, but it is possible for anyone else to also live by these maxims and seek to express these things as well. Along with this go other suggested actions according to Cormac, such as feeding orphans, giving good judgments, raising up the weak, quelling wrongs, and loving Truth while hating falsehood, all of which can be embraced by anyone seeking to live in honor. To seek to live these qualities is to seek to live Truth and support the right order of the world. The veracity of this statement is seen in the final passage where Cormac describes what will occur in the kingdom of a good king, should he follow all this advice. We see the description of a good king ruling over a fertile land, with oak trees full of acorns, fruitful earth and rivers full of fish. In the same way, if we as individuals seek to embody these characteristics and live these actions then we can also bring blessings upon the world we live in and make the quality of our own lives better.

Thoughts on the Testament of Morann

The Testament of Morann is the advice given to a king on how to rule well. At first glance this piece may seem simple and may also seem like something that doesn't apply to anyone not planning to rule, but in fact much wisdom can be gained from studying this text. The first section discusses the power of reciprocity and the benefits gained from holding to the ideal of Truth. The second section teaches the new king how to judge well and by what measure to judge all things. The final section discusses superior things and the four types of kingship. When taken as a whole these sections help us to see the right order of the world and how to maintain it.

It is important to understand why the first section looks at both the power of reciprocity and of the power of Truth, because although these two concepts are often viewed as separate, in reality they are expressions of one ideal. Reciprocity is the universal balance that is maintained; when we give we get in return. Truth is the equilibrium of the universe, it is the pivot point on which reciprocity rests. Each one exists as an expression of the other and neither could exist without the other. Within the text this is expressed through lines such as, 'Let him exalt mercy, it exalth him,' which teaches us that the characteristics we embody will in turn be drawn to us and, 'It is through the truth of the ruler that milk-yields of great cattle are maintained,' which shows us that it is through the manifestation of Truth that reciprocity yields positive things for the king's subjects. On a smaller scale this can be found to hold true within the lives of each individual and each Druid; when we speak and live Truth our lives will reflect blessings and we will draw to us the things we embody.

The second section focuses on the king's judgment of all things within his kingdom. At first glance this may seem superfluous to many of us, but in fact much wisdom is hidden in these lines, for the king is urged to judge all things by their own produce as we can see from lines like, 'Let him estimate the earth by its fruits'. This is good advice for anyone, because it urges us to judge anyone or anything only by the end product, surely a method to reach a fair and impartial judgment. If we seek to judge not through emotion nor based on the item or person themselves, but only on the result or product, then we will judge fairly and well.

The final section is the most poetic of the piece, opening with the lines:

Darkness yields to light
Sorrow yields to joy
An oaf yields to a sage
A fool yields to a wise man
A serf yields to a free man
Inhospitality yields to hospitality.

These also contain deep wisdom if studied. The first two lines set up our understanding of the rest of the wisdom we are shown, for indeed darkness yields to light and sorrow to joy by their own nature and just so does a fool yield to a wise man. This is not a statement about the intelligence of men or about the choices people make in different situations, but rather it is a commentary on the natural order of the world and how one condition or person yields to another. This segment then segues into a description of 15 characteristics that the king should have, followed by a list of ten things that 'extinguish' the rule of a bad king; when studied closely we can see that these ten are reciprocal benefits of the 15 things listed in the previous line, reinforcing that to exemplify certain characteristics is to draw blessings to our lives. The writer then proclaims that the king 'may die' and 'will die', and 'may depart' and 'will depart', but that what matters is how he rules for that is how he will be remembered. This is important advice for us all to remember, because we will all die one day and it is by our actions during life that we will be judged by those who come after us. Finally this last section discusses four types of rulers: the true ruler, the wily ruler, the oppressive ruler, and the bull ruler. We can also look at this in broader terms as describing four types of people in general; the one who lives by Truth, the one who lives by doing what is in their own best interests, the one who lives by force and outside control of others, and the one who is in constant conflict with others.

The Testament of Morann holds much wisdom for living as a good king, or as a good Druid. It shows us how to live in Truth, judge wisely, to seek the natural order, and describes the four types of rulers. Knowing all of this, it is up to us to choose which of the four types of people we want to strive to be. If we want to be a person who lives by Truth then this work gives us many of the tools to find that path and master the wisdom needed for it; in the end, whether we seek to be a good ruler, a good Druid, or a good person, all of these tools will be needed.

Modern Ethics for a Modern Druid

People sometimes wonder about modern Druidic ethics and how – or even if – the concept of 'harm none' fits in to a Druid's approach. Some people feel strongly that a modern Druid should adhere to an ethical view that avoids any harm to others, although it varies between avoiding all harm and avoiding harm to other people. In contrast, other people feel that modern Druids should preserve the best of the ancient Celtic views, including ethics.

My own opinion tends to agree with the second school of thought. I believe that as Druids in a modern world we are best served by, and we best serve, the ancient Druids' memory, by learning what the ancient Druids, and to a greater degree the Celts, believed and finding the best ways to adapt that to our own time. Otherwise our ethics are not those of Celtic polytheists or Druids, but simply modern (or post modern) ethics; this is neither right nor wrong in itself, but as Druids I believe our ethics should be those of Druids.

Let's begin by looking at some of what we know of the ancient Druids and of Celtic morality. There are several examples in Irish lore that support the idea that violence was seen as being a necessity at times. From the triads of Ireland: 'Three deaths that are better than life: the death of a salmon, the death of a fat pig, the death of a robber', and: 'Three bloodsheds that need not be impugned: the bloodshed of battle, of jealousy, of mediating'. (Meyers, 1906). Although the Brehon laws emphasize compensation over corporal punishment, the death penalty was a reality in Ireland. For example, in the case of a homicide if the person refused to go before a Brehon or if he could not or would not pay the levied fine then he could lawfully be killed (Joyce, 1908). No Brehon would ever order physical punishments, as paying a fine was the standard legal punishment for any crime, but nonetheless punishments including death and blinding were common (Joyce, 1908). What this tells us is that while the Druids themselves did not advocate violence in criminal cases, it was socially acceptable for such punishments to occur. The Druids also advised kings, and this included advising military actions from cattle raids in Ireland to rebelling against Rome in Gaul; and we know as well from Tacitus's account of the destruction of Anglesey that the Druids stood against the opposing army. Juxtaposing that, we also know that a Druid could stop a battle by walking between the two forces. Druids were expected to be wise enough to know when to encourage the action and when to stop it.

In fact, rather than violence, the main actions or traits that are condemned seem to be greed and lust. From the Triads of Ireland: 'The three chief sins: avarice, gluttony, lust.'(Meyers, 1906). A variety of the Brehon laws look at legislating states of marriage, sexual relations, and theft (I suggest reading Fergus Kelly's A Guide to Early Irish Law for more on this). According to Kelly's book, theft could be punishable by hanging (Kelly, 1988). In some of the existing prophecies relating to the future or end of the world, such as the one given by Ferchetne in the Colloquy of Two Sages or the Morrigan's prophecy in the Cath Maige Tuired, a lot of emphasis is placed on the lack of honor, lack of modesty, false judgments, lack of truth, and a general going against the natural order of things that will occur. Similarly the Testament of Morann and the Instructions of King Cormac mac Airt emphasizes the importance of the king manifesting Truth, good judgment, generosity, and moderate behavior in order to uphold the bounty and prosperity of the land; this included being ambitious, invading neighbors, and punishing criminals. In Celtic thought there was clearly a link between correct ethics and behavior and the success or failure of life and the world itself, but those ethics, in general, seem to be directed at preserving the correct order of the world rather than improving it or idealizing it. People are not urged to abstain from alcohol or sex, or even violence, but to engage in those things in moderation and within the socially correct context; only when the actions exceed social acceptance or defy social order are there consequences.

So how do I relate this to other pagan ethics? I think Druidism in general is closer ethically to other reconstructionist faiths such as Asatru, which emphasizes many of the same values. Although modern Druidry and Wicca share a common root in the friendship of Gerald Gardner and Ross Nichols, a Druidism based more in the Celtic culture would seem to reject the modern Wiccan ethic of the Rede; although I believe there is a valid argument for the similarity in spirit of the original Rede and Druidic ethics. The original Rede, after all, was not an absolute moral law but a guideline for behavior that was open to personal choice with an understanding of consequences (I highly recommend Peter Coughlin's book Ethics and the Craft for more on this subject). In the same way Celtic ethics appear to be based on the idea of personal responsibility and accepting the consequences of any action. However, the modern Rede as it is understood by many people is seen as less flexible and more absolute and would be difficult to harmonize with my understanding of Celtic ethics. The Celts seemed to have an understanding of harm as having a place within the greater workings and balance of the world, and I have a difficult time envisioning a Druidic ethic that advocates the lack of balance inherent in a path that rejects all harm. People are expected to accept the consequences of their own actions, even if that consequence is harmful to them. The natural world is expected to endure some harm in support of human life. Even nature itself includes a balance between harm and life that is normative; natural forest fires destroy yet also clear the way for new growth, and life is often predicated on some level of harm to other living things.

How do I personally incorporate Celtic ethics into my practice of Druidism? I believe that the ultimate lessons of such ethics are Truth and moderation, and so this is what I seek in my life. Truth is an understanding of the nature of reality and of living in correct alignment with that reality; when I manifest Truth in my life then I also manifest positive qualities in the world around me. Another aspect of this is good judgment, since a person who is embracing Truth should consequently be able to correctly understand the nature of other things and reach correct judgments about them. Moderation is another key aspect, where a person should be generous without being careless, ambitious without being over-reaching, and brave without being foolish, for example. How does this relate to causing harm? Well, I see harm as sometimes necessary – there are times when a tree must be cut down for the good of the other trees, or for a need; there are times when a small pain is needed to prevent a greater one later. And there are times when violence is necessary as well. I know myself well enough to know that if my children's lives were threatened I would do whatever I had to in order to protect them, and knowing this I could never say that I live my life with the belief of never harming another person. I would be hypocritical to say such a thing. Although a great deal of my life is directed at preserving life and healing those who need healing, I know that sometimes we must defend ourselves. Sometimes we must bring harm, but I try to never do so without a reason. My ethic embraces harm only as it is absolutely necessary; creating a dynamic that nurtures life and healing but accepts the balance that nature requires. If I harvest a plant it is for food or another use; I have taught my children never to recklessly destroy plants for fun. When I eat meat I appreciate the sacrifice of the animal's life – truly when I eat anything I appreciate the living thing that died to feed me. And if I have to harm a person intentionally I see it as a last resort and do so only if it seems justified. This all applies equally to physical actions and to magic. I feel that this is most strongly in line with the ancient Celtic ethics and also is in line with the modern world.

To me the most important part is being able to understand if there is a need for the harm, and being able to accept the consequences of my own actions. If I cause harm then I try to follow the old Brehon law consequence of making reparations; I acknowledge what I did or my part in what happened and seek to recompense the involved or affected person. I strive to preserve harmony and balance within my understanding of Truth.

References:

Joyce, P., (1908). A Smaller Social History of Ancient Ireland. Retrieved from http://www.alia.ie/tirnanog/sochis/sochis01.html#iv

Kelly, F., (1988). A Guide to Early Irish Law.

Meyers, K., (1906). The Triads of Ireland. Retrieved from http://www.ucc.ie/celt/online/T103006.html

Thoughts on the Uraicecht Na Riar

The Uraicecht Na Riar is an interesting text that deals with the different grades of poets in Ireland, what background and level of training each grade must have and what the honor price of each grade is. This is an important text to study because it can give us insight into the probable structure of the Druids themselves, and helps us to understand the important social position they held. For modern Druids this piece is useful to help show a viable structure that could be used to divide up different levels of knowledge within Druidism getting away from the standard, but probably less accurate, bard-ovate-Druid division.

The Uraicecht Na Riar begins by establishing that there are seven grades of poet and naming all of them beginning with the highest ranked the Ollam. The Ollam has advanced through the other grades, and has 350 compositions representing 50 for each grade of poet, and is a master of genealogy and the law. Because an Ollam has such extensive knowledge and represents the highest grade of poet his honor price of 40 sets is extremely high. The text also establishes the proper number of people in an Ollam's retinue under different circumstances.

This passage also tells us that a poet who is the son and grandson of poets has a higher honor price than one who isn't.

Such a statement reinforces two things: that the Irish did follow a type of caste system where children were born into the class of their parents, and also that this system was somewhat flexible based on talent. A person born into a family of poets had a higher honor price. However, a person born into a non-poetic family could still aim to become an Ollam based on skill and talent, although he would only command half the honor price. In modern terms this teaches us that anyone can become a Druid, but that respect should be given to those who are raised in Druidic families, especially as we move forward and more children are raised in such ways.

Next, and of particular interest, the Uraicecht Na Riar goes into detail on how a grade is conferred on a poet. The aspiring poet goes before the Ollam and shows his compositions, the number based on his grade, and the Ollam declares his grade based on these compositions and also that the poet is guiltless and pure; pure of learning, speech, 'hand', body, and guiltless of any crime. Once the Ollam has accepted the poet's work and declared him fit to his grade he brings him before the king who accepts the poet in this grade. This can be adapted to modern circumstances as the ritual acceptance of a new Druid, who should be tested by a senior Druid – preferably of the highest rank – and then presented to and accepted by the community.

The text goes on to describe each grade down from the Ollam, how many compositions and how much knowledge they should each have and what their honor price and retinue are. The next level down is the Anruth who has 125 tales and 25 to 50 stories. Next is the Cli with a third of the poetic art, and fourth is the Cano with a quarter of the tales. Next is the Dos with 1/5 of the poetic art, followed by the Macfuirmid with 40 compositions, then the Fochloc with 1/7 of the art. Then three more grades are listed as the basest of the bards described as unlettered and fools, equivalent to people with little or no skill and minimal learning. In a modern context we might say that the base three grades are uninitiated students, the Fochloc the newly initiated student and each grade up from that representing a more experienced Druid who has gained knowledge and skill and is advanced beyond the grades below.

The final sections of the Uraicecht look at specific aspects of the poetic art that deal with cursing and magic. The first example is a very blunt death spell, a spoken charm that asks for the target to die and be 'under the earth', and includes a caution that such death spells are why the nemed poets are so respected. The next section describes the proper way to enact a satire, or curse, using a sung or spoken charm, the turning of the moon, and action done against an effigy with a thorn from a Hawthorn tree.

Taken in its entirety this text offers not only a wonderful view of the Irish class of poets, but also some useful ideas for modern applications of the grade system and the use of satire. Even for those who choose not to use cursing under any circumstance, studying this aspect of the text is still a good way to gain an understanding of Irish Druidic magic. Although many groups choose to follow a more modern division of bards-ovates-Druids within their orders, this text presents an intriguing possible alternative that offers a more cohesive system where each Druid moves up in rank over time according to skill in a linear fashion instead of traveling a course through seemingly different focuses.

Thoughts on the Colloquy of the Two Sages

One of the most important texts for modern Druids to study may be the Colloquy of the Two Sages, the tale of a confrontation between the esteemed Druid Ferchertne and the recently graduated student Nede. The tale, on its surface, is a simple story of a confrontation sown by Bricriu between the elder and the youth after Bricriu convinces Nede, who is returning from training overseas, to seize a rank beyond his experience. The two Druids face off over the literal seat of contention, engaging in a battle of words and wits to test who truly deserves to sit there. In the end Ferchertne emerges the victor, but Nede's graceful defense earns him a place as Ferchertne's student.

Reading this story establishes a pattern of challenge and response that is useful for all modern Druids to study. Nede's initial actions are bold, even arrogant, as he assumes the chair of the highest ranked Druid in the land and this can be seen as the opening challenge in the coming confrontation. Nede does not approach Ferchertne as a humble petitioner, but rather by declaring his own value and assuming a place as if it were already his own. In response we see the first of Ferchertne's challenges, not only of words but of actions and attitude as he tests Nede's resolve and temper by speaking angrily and insulting Nede's experience and knowledge. Nede passes this challenge by responding calmly and proclaiming his own wisdom. This, then, sets the stage for the next phase of the testing, the direct question, where Ferchertne asks Nede where he is from, what his name is, what art he practices, what his tasks are, by what path has he come, whose son he is, and what tidings there are. None of these are direct, literal questions, but all are allegorical and are responded to with poetry, and each question is answered and then turned back on the elder Druid. It is only after the final question, where each man is asked to prophesy, that Nede concedes to Ferchertne and willingly proclaims him the better poet and seer and kneels at Ferchertne's feet, at which point the older Druid asks the younger to stay on as his student. From this we can see that the importance of the period of questioning and answering as a form of testing, as well as the importance of the final acknowledgements of the student's true place.

In modern Druidism this pattern of challenges could be used to model actual initiation rites on; it also illustrates the vital importance of two elements within modern traditions: the student-teacher relationship, and the hierarchy of wisdom. The traditional Druidic model of teaching, as illustrated in this Colloquy, shows a student petitioning to study with a teacher, studying with that person for as long as there is knowledge to be gained there, and then moving on to find a new teacher. This is illustrated in Nede's studying at first with Eochaid in Scotland and when that teacher can teach him no further he is sent back to Ireland where the main action of the tale between Nede and Ferchertne occurs. This is a useful model to be used today as well. The story also illustrates the importance of understanding our individual place within the greater hierarchy of our fellow Druids and both respecting those above us as well as teaching those beneath us.

I, personally, found a great deal of beauty and inspiration in this story. The question about what art they practice gives a list of the many skills the Druids claimed including satire, blessing, poetic inspiration, storytelling, peacemaking, and teaching wisdom. The tale also showed me something of the proper balance of attitude that Druids were expected to have, both proud and assertive but also respectful and quick-witted in the face of confrontation. Nede serves as a great model to meditate on as a student who is well on the way to earning fame and a place of honor. I can hold Nede before me as an example of how to react to a challenge and how to carry myself with pride while still remaining respectful of those wiser than I.

On a final note, the Colloquy is also a treasure trove of cultural references and Druidic lore that anyone interested in Druidism should take the time to study. I favor Christian Guyonvarc'h's book The Making of a Druid: Hidden Teachings from the Colloquy of the Two Sages because of the detailed and extensive introduction, notes, and appendices. Being able to study the story with the different translations and glosses included is very useful and illuminating, and offers additional insight into some of the passages. These additions, such as the extensive discussion about the seven poetic grades, are an important aspect to understand for both Druids and Celticists, or anyone else interested in Irish culture.

Thoughts on the Article 'The Excellence of Ancient Word'

The Excellence of Ancient Word by Sean Tuathail is a work which should be essential reading for any Druid or anyone studying Druidism. This work is important on several levels: it gives us a description of a Druid based on Irish sources, it shows us the importance of Druids within society, and it shows us one type of magic employed by Druids. All three of these things are important in helping us form a picture of who the ancient Druids were and in helping us to create a viable modern Druidic path.

The article describes the Irish Druids as wearing 'rainbow' cloaks (Kellnhauser, 1993), a fact that is supported by other sources such as those mentioned in the article on Druidic clothing and dress by Searles O'Dubhain (O'Dubhain, 1999). This knowledge invites us to search further and as we research we learn more about the social codes that defined the different classes and decided who could wear which colors. The description of the Druid's cloak being 'rainbow' colored reflected the Druid's right to wear six colors, the second most allowed beneath only the king who could wear seven (O'Dubhain, 1999). The article also describes the Druid as wearing a feathered cloak, another detail that is supported elsewhere, although in other sources the feathers are said to be on the cloak (O'Dubhain, 1999). Beyond the physical description the article also supports the importance of trees that vary from the popular and well-known British oak and parasitic mistletoe: these are the rowan, yew, and hazel (Kellnhauser, 1993). These trees were of primary importance to the Irish Druids, but are often overshadowed by the more well known English tree and plant. For the modern Druid seeking to follow an Irish path this knowledge is very important to have, and to work with.

The article also reinforces the social position of the Druids themselves. As the aforementioned right to wear certain colors illustrates, from a social standpoint Druids ranked second only to the king in what they had the right to wear. In other ways, such as the rights to cross borders and to receive premiere hospitality, the Druidic poets actually exceeded the power of kings (Kellnhauser, 1993). This should demonstrate the vital importance of Druids within Irish society; so important that even kings could be laid low by an offended Druid. By studying the privileges afforded to Druids and the respect with which they were treated we can also come to have a better understanding of their place within their society and, in turn, the place we should strive to earn within our own modern society. In our world we are not given this respect merely for being a Druid, but we can make it a goal to earn that same level of respect through our actions, and in so doing renew the respect given to the title of Druid itself.

Finally the article goes into depth discussing one particular style of Druidic magic, the extemporaneous spoken spell, or roscanna (Kellnhauser, 1993). The roscanna is a special type of charm that is usually composed as it is spoken and has magical power to influence the topic of the poem (Kellnhauser, 1993). One of the most famous examples of a roscanna is the Song of Amergin, which is a spell of power and of claiming the land, and the first volley in the battle between the Milesans and Tuatha Dé Danann (Kellnhauser, 1993). Dissecting each of the roscanna is beyond the scope of this essay, but it is a useful exercise for those interested in the practice of spoken Celtic magic. Taking all of them as a whole we can see the common pattern of the Druid speaking from a place of power to declare what will occur with the confidence that this declaration will then come to pass. This teaches us the importance of a Druid speaking in such a way when casting magic, but also acts as a caution for any Druid to guard their words lest what they declare does indeed come to pass. Roscanna are also often vehicles of prophecy, which adds another interesting aspect to them.

In conclusion, this article expands our view of Druids by showing us different aspects of them not often discussed in other sources and it acts as a great springboard to encourage further inquiry. Reading this we learn more about how Druids appeared in the ancient world as well as how they would have been treated by their contemporaries. The article also teaches us a great deal about roscannas and can act as the first step for those seeking to begin practicing that style of magic. This knowledge can serve to expand the picture of Druids to those learning about them and will deepen the practice of modern Druids as well.

References:

Kellnhauser, J., (1993). The Excellence of Ancient Word: Druid Rhetorics from Ancient Irish Tales. Retrieved from http://www.imbas.org/articles/excellence_of_the_ancient_word.html

O'Dubhain, S., (1999). Druidic Clothing and Dress. Retrieved from http://www.summerlands.com/crossroads/library/druidic_clothing%20_and_dress.htm

Hear My Prayer

There's a saying in neopaganism, 'Ask three pagans a question and you'll get five answers.' Well, I think if you ask three neopagans about prayer you may get seven answers. It always surprises me that something that seems so essential to me can cause so much controversy in the larger neopagan community; after all prayer can be found (as far as I know) in every culture and religion around the world. Yet there are some people who are very firm in their opinions that prayer has no place in neopaganism. The same is true in reconstructionism although I've seen it more in heathenry than CR. There just seems to be something about prayer – especially daily or devotional prayer – that really puts some people off. Now don't get me wrong, I'm all in favor of personal practice being unique and I don't think what works for me should be required for anyone else; I may pray daily and someone else may never pray outside ritual, or at all, and that's fine. What I don't understand is people who are totally against the concept altogether.

There seems to be some idea that prayer, daily or devotional prayer that is, is a 'Christian thing', despite the fact that it is seen in many other cultures. I am not as open about this as I used to be because when I talk about it I almost inevitably am accused of having Christian baggage – hilarious since I wasn't raised Christian and only studied Christianity as an adult long after my habit of daily prayer was begun. But the whole 'Christian baggage' thing is a common accusation in some pagan and reconstructionist debates, tossed out without any supporting argument, and used as if it were the final word. The equivalent of saying, 'No one should listen to you because you think like one of *them*'; like a child shouting, 'You have cooties!'

Personally I love prayer; I pray in the mornings and I pray at night because I find it helps me feel both connected to Powers beyond myself – be they my ancestors, the daione sidhe, or the Gods – and that I get a feeling of peace and centered-ness from prayer. I pray because I want to pray and because I enjoy praying. Prayer is a little way, on a regular basis, to strengthen and reaffirm my relationship with those Powers. I may accompany my prayers with little offerings – incense, candles, herbs, actions – or I may only offer my own energy. I tend to follow the Celtic practice of singing my prayers, making little chants and songs out of traditional material I have reworked or writing my own. I may pray to ask for things like protection for my home and family or blessings, or I may just pray to honor whoever I am praying to. I try to have fun with it; I once even made a prayer in limerick form. I feel like I am giving my energy and focus to those Powers for that time and I also feel like I am getting something out of it because it does help me feel better and more connected to them.

There is a lot of beauty in prayer that I wish more people were open to, even if they don't choose to do it.

Lorica Prayers

Lorica is a Latin word for a soldier's leather breastplate or corselet; in Christian tradition it was a prayer said for protection every day. There is a very well known Lorica prayer in Irish tradition, called Saint Patrick's Breastplate. I very much like the idea of this type of prayer and think that it adapts well to pagan use. I also think that it can help enrich and deepen our spiritual practice to have daily prayers we say to connect to things beyond ourselves and maintain the reciprocal relationship we have with the Spirits around us. I believe the Lorica prayer – perhaps we could call it cathéide in Irish, which means armor – is a great thing to include in these daily prayers. In my own personal version I have blended the idea somewhat with the ideas seen in the Song of Amergin of relating to the many different parts of creation. Being that it is so personal I'm not comfortable making my own daily Lorica prayer public but I will share another Lorica prayer I wrote. Perhaps it will be useful for others, or serve as inspiration for you to write your own.

A Modern Irish Pagan's Lorica

I arise today in joy
Through the strength of the sea,
Stability of the strong earth,
Endlessness of the eternal sky.
I bind to myself
The endurance of my ancestors,
The eloquence of the poets,
The truth of the ancient Druids.
I bind to myself
The speed of the hawk
The courage of the deer

The wisdom of the salmon.
I bind to myself
The inspiration of the Gods
The mystery of the Otherworld
The illumination of Spirit
I summon today all these powers
between me and any dangers
Every day that I recite this prayer
I am protected from harm
In the names of my Gods
and by sea, earth, and sky.

Belief and Practice

There seems to be a pervasive, underlying dualism in paganism which can be seen in the various either/or arguments that go around. Either religion or spirituality; either modern or traditional; and, at the moment, either belief or practice. It should come as no surprise to anyone who knows me and my liminal ways that I reject both hard views – the either/or paradigm – and instead my own perspective is based in balance.

The current discussion going around is centered on whether it is orthodoxy (belief) or orthopraxy (practice) that matters more. One view holds that belief is the cornerstone to everything else and that what we do is less important than what we believe; by this view community is built on a similarity of belief. We all believe the same therefore we are all the same religion. In contrast the other view holds that what we believe is less important than what we do and that community is based on a similarity of practice. We do the same thing, ritually; therefore we are the same religion. The belief argument is often held as a neopagan stance, while the practice side is held by reconstructionists. Both have their pros and cons; similar belief can acts as common ground for those with different practices, while similar practice can act as common ground for those with different beliefs.

My sticking point in all of this is the either/or aspect, the idea that it has to be one way or the other. I believe this is a logical fallacy, a false dilemma. My experience with the pagan community over the last few decades has shown me that those who hold to the orthodoxy view still have boundaries of acceptable and unacceptable practice, just as the orthopraxy side has limits to what beliefs are and are not allowed. Most neopagan groups, for example, that embrace the idea of similar belief will still reject practices that involve, say, conducting a mass to the Goddess in the guise of Mary, even if they all believe that Mary is a face of the Goddess. Similarly the orthopraxy groups will reject beliefs that are too far out of the accepted norm, such as CR groups that refuse to allow CR style worship to Lwa. (Note that these examples are purely illustrative and not meant to imply any personal judgment in any direction). The point is that it is not nearly as clear cut or simple as the either/or. To be heathen or CR is as much about believing in the deities and cosmology – on some level – as it is practicing like everyone else. Even atheist heathens relate to the Gods in some way and understand the heathen worldview. So to my mind it isn't either belief or practice, its belief *and* practice.

If I had to concisely describe my own view I suppose I would say that it is experiential, because experiencing something beyond ourselves – whether that experience comes through belief or practice – seems to me to be the heart of spirituality. Rote belief or practice by themselves, to me, are not transformative or powerful, but can be tools to reach past ourselves and create that connection. Even if the experience is a simple moment, an awareness that we didn't have before, it is that experience that we should strive for. Of course I am coming from a very esoteric place and my own past experiences shape my views on the value of experience; it may well be different for everyone else, and I don't judge those who find true value without transformative experiences. Spirituality will always be unique in many ways to the individual practicing it, no matter how much common ground that person shares with their community.

I am a wanderer, and sometimes I practice with those who hold different beliefs just as sometimes I practice differently from those with similar beliefs. I do not feel that having a different belief from someone is an insurmountable issue, nor that practicing differently is the core of what defines us. A community is too diverse to ever fit into such a narrow model. No, it will always be a blend of differences and similarities, with a fine balance maintaining the homeostasis necessary for the community to exist at all. Sometimes people stray too far from the common belief or the common practice and cross that boundary of 'acceptable' and then a new community is formed, but generally even in communities that emphasize orthopraxy or orthodoxy there will always be variations. It's human nature.

Ritual Structure

All ritual, at its heart, should serve the dual purposes of honoring the Gods and of opening us to their blessing. It should also allow us to be aware of and reflect on our connection to those Powers and our part in the natural and cosmic cycles. It is said, although I can't lay my hands on the exact reference right now, that the ancient Druids believed that their rituals were a perpetual act of creation that kept the cosmos going; I like to think that even today our rituals help keep cosmic order, if only because it nurtures my own feeling of connection to everything. Now personally I use several different ritual styles, depending on context. In public rituals I tend to use a more general neopagan format because it is the most accessible to the most people, and my community is comprised mostly of diverse neopagans. I have found that going with what people recognize and are familiar with creates the best results for the participant in an 'open' public format (not that I don't work in some of my own bits, like having a public group walk between two candles representing bonfires during a Beltane ritual). I'm perfectly comfortable using this format myself in any of its variations and I believe that public rituals should be based in what the group connects best with. I am out there, after all, to serve my community, not myself. Other people have their own views on the subject, of course, this is just mine.

Now with my kindred we tend to use a basic blot structure. Sometimes we use the hammer hallowing beforehand, sometimes we don't, but we always start by hailing the ancestors, land spirits, and Gods, pouring out offerings from the horn to each. We go around after they are hailed and we each say what we want or need to about why we are gathered and may make additional offerings. When we have all said as much as we feel we need to we take the collected offerings out and pour them onto our outdoor altar space, called a ve, while thanking the Gods and spirits for their blessings. Then we feast, usually a pot-luck style meal together (some of this food is also offered later).

As an Irish pagan and Druid, when I do rituals it's usually just me, or me and my children. I try to follow a basic recon-style approach, but I have the freedom to improvise a little bit as well, even within the set structures of the specific traditions I work in. This is just a basic outline for home rituals, and this is only the way that I do things, although it reflects my understanding of reconstruction style ritual and some general principles behind the ritual style of the groups I belong to. Basically this is my disclaimer that I'm not trying to put this out there as any sort of set ritual format for anyone but myself. Of course the groups I belong to do have specific set ritual structures, but that's not what I'm writing about, nor is it necessarily my place to do so.

I start off by burning juniper, vervain, or an incense blend I make that combines several herbs and woods used historically for cleansing. I like to sing, so I usually sing something that creates a feel of ritual or sacredness – at the moment I've been going with the song There Is No Time, which I learned from the pagan singer Kellianna; it's not historic or even tradition specific, but I like it and I feel it works to create the energy I want to start off with. While I sing I walk three times sunwise around my ritual space, sometimes carrying the incense. After this I acknowledge the three realms and the three Powers associated with them; sea and the ancestors, land and the daoine sidhe, sky and the Gods. If a specific holy day or occasion is associated with one or two deities then I will only call that one or those two when calling the Gods. I invoke[1] each Power and make offerings to them appropriate to their nature and which are environmentally safe. For example, I might offer incense made from organic local plants, I might light a candle, I might write a poem and then burn the only copy during ritual, I might burn butter or olive oil, I might pour out pure water, milk, cream, or (rarely) alcohol, that sort of thing. After all the guests have been invited to the party, so to speak, I will talk a little about the purpose of the rite, perhaps read a poem or blessing – often something traditional from a source like the Carmina Gadelica, sometimes modernized or made pagan. If I know any appropriate songs I would sing them now. Some specific holy days like Beltane or Samhain have particular actions or activities that might occur, while others are more general. This is when any special activity or prayers would be done, followed by divination to assess if the offerings were accepted and the actions effective. If the divination indicates a problem I will try to narrow down what the issue is and correct it, usually with additional offerings. Assuming the divination looks good and nothing has to be redone or 'fixed' then the main body of the rite is finished. The gathered Powers are acknowledged and thanked for their presence (except the daoine sidhe, as I have a superstition about never saying 'thank you' to them; I ask instead that there always be friendship and peace between us). The energy of the ritual is grounded as an offering to the earth, and any physical offerings are poured out on the ground or left outside on the outdoor altar. Usually this is followed by feasting.

There is a lot of similarity between the heathen style ritual and the Irish/Druid style one, but the heathen blot tends to be simpler and more straightforward, an honoring of the Gods and Spirits. Druid ritual is a bit more about energy and the altered consciousness that comes from connecting to Powers outside ourselves, in my experience. And public ritual should create some feeling of connection and experience while honoring the Gods. All rely on a basic structure blended with unique elements and a person's willingness to be open in giving (making offerings) and receiving (accepting blessings/experiences).

Offerings and Sacrifice

One of the key aspects of practice when using a reconstructionist approach is the idea of offerings and sacrifice. It comes up in discussion on groups all the time, both people discussing what the ideas mean to them and also talking about what constitutes an acceptable offering or sacrifice. As with everything there are many different opinions on the subject.

For myself I define a sacrifice as the giving to a Power something precious and valuable – often irreplaceable – and I see an offering as the giving of something special but not unique. Put another way I see a sacrifice as a gift while an offering is more of a sharing. These are purely my own definitions of course; if you look both words up in the dictionary you'll see the meanings are essentially identical. When the subject of sacrifices comes up people usually think of animals, but other things like jewelry, silver, and weaponry can also be sacrificed. Offerings might include incense, flowers, food, candles, drink, a gift of skill like a poem or anything along those lines. I make offerings very regularly, but I have only once made a sacrifice; I sacrificed a sword to the waters for the Morríghan. Sacrifices, to me, are a pretty big deal, which is why I've only ever made the one.

Offerings can be intense and important as well, so I always trust my intuition to help me decide what to give.

Everyone has their own opinions on when and why to make offerings, and make no mistake some people take it very, very seriously. Everyone, even if they follow a similar path, can have different views and expectations on this subject, but I think it's always important to trust your own gut. Let your own connection to deity – or whoever you are offering to – guide you. Whatever path you follow you'll get a feel for what offerings are considered usual to give in different situations and it's always good to ask around if you aren't sure, but in the end you're the one offering it so it's your decision. Sometimes you may feel that you shouldn't give an offering – the Havamal says, 'Better no prayer than too big an offering.' (Verse 146, Bellows trans.) – and that's alright too.

I think that an offering should come from a genuine place; it shouldn't be a bribe or an attempt to buy an outcome from the Gods, at least not in my view. There is certainly the aspect to offerings where they were seen as something to be given when asking for something, but still, I see this less as a 'payment' if you will and more as an exchange of energy, 'a gift for a gift' (Havamal 146, Bellows). After all when you pay for something you expect a specific result and making an offering, or sacrifice, doesn't guarantee anything, but on the same hand it's generally considered polite to offer something when asking a Power for anything. When I make offerings at seasonal rites they are not given to ensure something so much as to give thanks for what I already have been given and to honor the Powers. It is said that the ancient Druids believed that their ceremonies contributed to the perpetual act of creation that kept the universe going and I can see that as well, how offerings keep reinforcing the bonds that hold everything together.

Basically, much like prayer, I make offerings because I want to not because I feel like I have to; they come from a place of connection and caring not obligation.

This is all just my thoughts on what sacrifices and offerings are, I'm sure most people will have their own opinions on the subject…

Pagan Piety

There is probably no faster way to start a fight on a pagan discussion board than to bring up the subject of piety in any form. For some reason the topic itself seems to immediately put people on the defensive, as if even discussing it is implicitly judging everyone. If I could have one wish relating to how the pagan community interacts among itself (hey a girl can dream) I think I would wish that each individual would stop judging everyone else based on what works for the individual.

For example if you bring up the topic of devotions on a discussion group, instead of an actual discussion about devotional practices it frequently and quickly devolves into more-pagan-than-thou pissing matches. Not everyone sinks to this level, but inevitably someone will comment on how essential frequent devotions are and someone else will react by accusing anyone who does devotional work of having Christian baggage, and then it just becomes a big argument. There doesn't seem to be any respect for the natural variation that occurs within any community; no acknowledgement that with such a personal thing as connection to the Gods and spirits what works for one person may be useless for another. And it doesn't seem to matter at all how valuable the practice is for the people who like it, which makes no sense to me. I understand discussing how historically accurate something is or how a practice fits into reconstruction, but the idea of ignoring evidence in support of something and condemning a practice entirely as 'unpagan' just because the speaker doesn't like it is ridiculous.

This is also seen a lot when the subject of dedication to a deity comes up. Within the pagan community you'll see the full range, from people who aren't sure the Gods exist and only acknowledge them on holy days, to those who feel enough of an affinity to a deity to dedicate themselves to that Power. Actually even within the sub-culture of those who have chosen to dedicate there can be a lot of judgment based on each individual's definition of what dedication means. But one way or another it always seems to come back to some people feeling threatened by others who do things differently, as if the other people's different practice is a judgment on the individual's own piety. Someone who only acknowledges the Gods in ritual is no more or less 'right' than one who is fully dedicated to a deity – the relationships are just different ways to connect to deity based on what works for that individual (and of course what the Gods want from them). In the same way a CR who does daily devotionals to the Gods and spirits is no more or less right than one who doesn't.

None of this is to say that there aren't legitimate issues within the subject of piety that are worth arguing over; however, it seems like whenever the subject comes up people lose all perspective and let their own bias take over. The community might judge our actions to decide how well or poorly we fit into the community, but in the end it is the Gods and spirits themselves who will decide the value of our efforts.

Piety isn't a competition to see who can get the most God-brownie-points, it's a way to live in right relation with the Gods and spirits around us. And, however tribal my overall view of religion is, when you get down to it how we each individually relate to those Gods and spirits is unique to each of us. Actions are meaningless if they are being done without the right intention or as empty duty, and not doing what we feel moved to do out of piety because of community judgment also detracts from our connection to deity.

For my own part I think the most important factor is the spirit any action for the Gods is done in, because piety, true piety, is the inner motivation that guides us. Although there can be value in pushing through spiritual dry periods by continuing to practice even when we aren't feeling very connected, in general I don't think we should do what we do not feel in our hearts nor should we hesitate to act when we feel called to if we want to build a real connection to Powers outside ourselves.

So I will end this with a quote to contemplate:

> *Are you not aware that all offerings whether great or small that are brought to the Gods with piety have equal value, whereas without piety, I will not say hecatombs, but, by the Gods, even the Olympian sacrifice of a thousand oxen is merely empty expenditure and nothing else?*
> Emperor Flavius Claudius Julianus the Pious and the Philosopher

With the Sun or Against the Sun

My reaction to things moving counterclockwise is something of a running joke among my friends, whether it's papers being passed around during a discussion group or a shared box of cookies passing from hand to hand. I suppose it does seem rather silly, since without any intent there's likely no harm in it, but I was raised with it drilled into me that movement clockwise, 'with the sun', is blessing and movement counterclockwise, or 'against the sun', is for cursing. It's funny how deeply ingrained these things can become over time, although I'm glad it gives my friends some amusement to watch me twitch and bite my tongue when the plate of brownies gets passed the 'wrong' way.

My feeling about directionality of movement is based on older ideas from Celtic culture, where direction was an important indicator of intent and could be used for blessing or cursing. This concept is largely non-existent in American culture, but can be seen with even a preliminary study of Celtic culture. I believe that it is important for modern practitioners of any Celtic faith to have at least a basic understanding of the importance of this subject and its principles.

F. Marian McNeill in volume 1 of her Silver Bough series discusses the different directions in Scottish tradition, which she refers to as the 'airts'. She relates each of the compass direction points to a season starting with spring in the east and moving clockwise around to the north. Additionally she mentions that this progression was seen as being connected to the path of the sun through the sky, but that she believes this clockwise movement may also connect to the constellation of Ursa Major. This constellation, which is also called the Farmer's Clock, points in each of the directions in the corresponding season. According to McNeill, clockwise, or deiseal, movement is always seen as good luck and positive while moving against the sun is viewed as unlucky and 'evil'. She relates that the Druids in their rituals moved clockwise, while witches 'danced tuaithiuil' (counter-clockwise) and that in the past warriors approaching a fort would walk either clockwise or counterclockwise to indicate whether they were friend or enemy. In particular she emphasizes the practice of walking three times clockwise around a space for blessing:

> *Expectant mothers went thrice round a church to ensure a safe delivery; fire was carried thrice round an infant before baptism to save it from the fate of a changeling; at a wedding, the company went thrice round the house before entering; sick persons thrice circulated a holy well before drinking the healing water; boats putting out to sea thrice rowed about sunwise in order to ensure a safe passage or a good catch; even coffins were carried thus to the grave.*
> (McNeill, 1956).

In the Carmina Gadelica we see several references to actions being done in specific directions for either blessing or cursing in Scotland. In one of the Hogmanay prayers we see a reference to a house being blessed by a group of singers walking around it clockwise, and likewise being cursed by the group walking around it counterclockwise while reciting a malediction. The emphasis on the actions makes it clear that it is not the words alone that have power but the words and the actions together.

In Dáithí O hÓgain's book the Sacred Isle the author discusses the Irish belief surrounding the power of going with or against the sun and the related beliefs of the relative goodness or badness of both the right and the left hands, and south and north. As he explains, when facing the rising sun a person's right hand is to the south-side, both then being associated with positive energy, while the left hand is to the north making both associated with going against the sun and the negative. Even the words for these things in Irish relate to these concepts:

> *In Irish the word deas and its derivatives are used in the sense of both 'south' and 'fortunate', whereas the word tuath and its derivatives are used to mean both 'north' and 'dangerous'.*
> (O hÓgain, 1999).

Like McNeill, hÓgain also connects the idea of warriors turning in different directions as significant, mentioning that in literature a warrior might turn to the right to bring good fortune while turning to the left indicated a threat to his enemies. Positive magic was done by turning or circling to the right, while cursing and destructive magic involved turning to the left. Even Saint Maodhog was said to have cursed two men by turning his sandals around to the left three times against them; and a very simple but enduring belief was that a person could be cursed by turning a stone in your hand counterclockwise against them. In Ireland, as well as Scotland, the custom is to walk clockwise around a healing well before approaching it.

In short it is a deeply ingrained idea in the Irish and Scottish tradition that certain directions have associations and that to move in a direction – with or against the sun – is significant. Go with the sun to bring luck and blessing, whether it is walking around a well or sacred place, or stirring your food as you cook. And when you need to curse someone... well... go the other way.

References:

Carmichael, A., (1900). Carmina Gadelica volume 1
McNeill, F., (1959). The Silver Bough volume 1
O hÓgain, D., (1999). The Sacred Isle

Druids and the Soul

What do we know about the Celts' and Druids' beliefs about the afterlife? Let's begin by looking at the secondary sources that we have, which generally agree with each other. Polyhistor wrote, 'The Pythagorean doctrine prevails among the Gauls' teaching that the souls of men are immortal, and that after a fixed number of years they will enter into another body.' This is echoed by Diodorus who wrote, 'The teachings of Pythagoras prevails among the Gauls, that the souls of humans are immortal and that after a certain number of years they live again, with the soul passing into another body.' (Freeman, 2002).

Valerius Maximus stated, 'They lent sums of money to each other which are repayable in the next world, so firmly are they convinced that the souls of men are immortal.'

Speaking of the Gauls, Pomponius Mela tells us:

> *One of their dogmas has come to common knowledge, namely, that souls are eternal and that there is another life... and it is for this reason too that they burn or bury with their dead things appropriate to them in life, and that in times past they even used to defer the completion of business and the payments of debts until their arrival in another world. Indeed there were some of them who flung themselves willingly on the funeral piles of their relatives in order*

to share the new life with them.
(Freeman, 2002).

Caesar wrote, 'The cardinal teaching of the Druids is that the soul does not perish, but after death pass from one body to another. Because of this teaching that death is only a transition, they are able to encourage fearlessness in battle.'

Lucan, in his poem Pharsalia, mocks this belief of the Druids, saying:

And it is you who say that the shades of the dead seek not the silent land of Erebus and the pale halls of Pluto; rather you tell us that the same spirit has a body again elsewhere, and that death, if what you sing is true, is but the midpoint of a long life.
(Matthews, 1998).

Where it gets tricky, of course, is discussing where exactly the soul goes between lives. In the Irish belief it can get very complex, with many different options, often referred to as 'Islands in the West', being possible. From stories we find in the Fairy Faith, and even depending on how we choose to view stories like that of Ossain and Naimh, a person may join the fairies (the daione sidhe) for example, or their spirit may otherwise wander, as Irish myth has an abundance of wandering souls to be found. Of course these examples are largely from much later periods and seeing them in relation to or connected to older beliefs is purely modern supposition. It is difficult to know what the ancient Celts may have believed about where the soul went between lives, for all that we do seem to have decent evidence that they did believe in the soul's continuance. My own approach is a synthesis of the ancient evidence and the modern Celtic cultural beliefs, particularly those of the Fairy Faith minus the Christian bits, so I tend to study and incorporate both, and it usually works out that they flow together seamlessly. I offer the material I use in my own practice here for readers to keep or discard as they choose.

Several different Irish myths discuss the topic of the immortal soul including the story of Tuan mac Cairill in the Lebor na hUidre. In this story Tuan mac Cairill tells the tale of Ireland from the beginning, which he has witnessed throughout his various lives as a man, then as a stag, a wild boar, an eagle, a salmon, and then a man again. As he says in the story, 'My name is Tuan son of Carell. But once I was called Tuan son of Starn, son of Sera, and my father, Starn, was the brother of Partholan.' While this is obviously a storytelling device, it may also hint at a belief in the continuity of the soul during the rebirth process. It is interesting food for thought anyway.

My own viewpoint is that the soul does reincarnate after a period of rest. We can never really judge how long a period in our world because time moves differently in the Otherworlds. I also think that when a person dies there are different possibilities for where their soul may go, depending on what the person believed, where they want to go, and how they lived their lives. Some may go to a period of rest in a land of peace, some may join their own ancestors, some may stay in this world as a guardian spirit or as a ghost. And I think that a soul after death is not greatly different than a soul before death, except that it has more access to the supernatural worlds that we as incarnate people have to work to connect to; this may be why people have traditionally gone to the dead to learn the future.

In the end the evidence does seem to support a Celtic and Druidic belief in the immortality of the soul and of the soul's rebirth. Much may be inferred from the secondary sources and mythology, but ultimately it will be up to the individual to decide how to fill in the details that are missing, such as where the soul goes between lives and for how long, and even to decide what value this belief will have for the individual.

References:

Freeman, P., (2002). War, Women, and Druids
Matthews, J., (1998). The Druid's Sourcebook http://www.sacred-texts.com/neu/celt/mlcr/mlcr03.htm
http://www.druidcircle.org/library/index.php?title=Celtic_Karma

The Magic of the Head and Hair

Well it wouldn't be the pagan community without some sort of drama, but I have to admit the current issue-de-jour sort of baffles me – because it's over head coverings in paganism. Basically there is a movement going in support of pagans who choose to veil or cover their heads, and this has caused a strong backlash among some people.

Personally? I think that each individual should decide for themselves what they want to do about covering or not covering their hair. I can't really understand the level of outrage some people feel about this issue, but it has also made me think more about my own views of the head, hair, and veiling.

I do not veil except when doing spae-work (oracular seidhr). To me putting on that veil is a mental cue that I am about to get oracular and since I don't want to be tranced out and predicting for strangers in Walmart I reserve veils for specific circumstances. I found it very interesting to see people discussing using head coverings and veils to block chakras or protect the head, as mine clearly has the opposite purpose. It makes me think that, as with many things, it is the intent and belief that matter most.

Contemplating the subject also had me thinking about the related issues of the head and hair. Now in Celtic belief the head is the seat of personal power; the heads of enemies or rivals who were defeated in battle could be taken as trophies, symbolizing the taking of that person's power. Related to that a defeated enemy's hair might be cut short to represent their loss of power; short hair was considered shameful (Irish Fireside, 2011).

Similarly in the Norse the hair of servants was cropped short, while people of higher rank wore their hair longer (Viking Answer Lady, 2012). In Ireland both men and women wore their hair long and loose, and women with long hair were considered particularly beautiful (Joyce, 1913). Interestingly the Anglo-Normans found this practice of loose hair to be barbaric and condemned it (Irish Fireside, 2011). In the Norse, an unmarried girl wore her hair loose, while a married woman braided hers, although a married woman might also wear a head covering (Viking Answer Lady, 2012). Hair styles clearly have a long history of being used to denote social rank and status. I had read – although I cannot now remember where – that when doing magic the hair was left loose so that the magic would not be caught in the braiding, and also that during labor all knots were untied and the mother's hair left loose to encourage an easier birth. Clearly this symbolized the connection between the hair and power, which was free when the hair was loose and bound when the hair was tied.

My own take on this? I wear my hair long as a symbol of personal power. This is both as a nod to the ancient Irish practice and as a personal reclaiming of power; as a child I was forced to wear my hair very short, an experience that most decidedly made me feel powerless. In my own practice I habitually let my hair down or unbraid it whenever I am doing serious magic. Whether or not this has any actual merit to it, it acts as a sign to my mind that I'm about to do some Work. And of course I wear a veil when doing spae. This is all just my own personal preference and practice, what I do to trigger certain states of mind, and how I view the relationship of hair to the power of the head. What other people do is truly up to them, as far as I'm concerned.

References:

Irish Fireside (2011). All About that Celtic Hair. http://irish-fireside.com/2011/08/25/all-about-that-celtic-hair/

Joyce, P., (1913). A Smaller Social History of Ireland. http://www.alia. ie/tirnanog/sochis/xviiia.html Viking Answer Lady (2012). Courtship, Love and Marriage in Viking Scandinavia and Viking Age Hairstyles, Haircare and personal grooming. Retrieved http://www.vikinganswer lady.com/wedding.shtml and http://www.vikinganswerlady .com/hairstyl.shtml

Chapter 2

Gods and Spirits

Celtic Deities

When we talk about Celtic deities we are really lumping together deities from the different Celtic cultures – generally Irish, Welsh, and Gaulish. This can sometimes give the false impression that these Gods are interchangeable or that they form a single cohesive pantheon, when in reality each culture had its own often unique deities that were worshipped. Since I follow a reconstructionist approach I tend to primarily honor one pantheon, the Irish, therefore the information I'm providing in this chapter, for the most part, will focus on the deities that I personally honor. I strongly suggest that anyone interested in Celtic paganism or Druidism similarly find one cultural pantheon that is the most appealing to them and learn about those Gods.

I tend to favor a more focused relationship with a few deities instead of the common modern 'cafeteria' approach to honoring the pagan Gods. I believe it is better to nurture a relationship with one or two specific deities associated with the activities or energies a person is interested in rather than looking up a name based on one association when a specific need arises. Most of the Gods are very multifunctional and can be prayed to for a variety of purposes.

There are many different ways to approach connecting to the Gods including a client-type relationship, devotional work, offerings, setting up an altar for the deity, and establishing the expectations and boundaries of the relationship. A client-type relationship approaches worship as a contract where the person agrees to certain terms, such as giving specific offerings, and requests the deity to fulfill a certain role. Divination may be used to see if the contract is accepted and then the relationship proceeds from this basis. In devotional work a person might dedicate themselves to a particular deity or group of deities and would then pray to and honor that deity regularly. Sometimes devotional work may be temporary to get to know a deity, if you will, and other times it may be a more permanent situation. For example I dedicated myself to the Morrignae for a specific period of time, but when that time was over I found a deeper more permanent dedication to Macha (one of the three Morrignae) had naturally evolved during the temporary period. With any deity offerings can be made to honor that Power, to give thanks, or to make a specific request. In the same way a small shrine or altar may be set up for that God or Goddess to serve as a focal point for honoring that Power. However it is done, it is a good idea to clearly set up the boundaries and expectations you have with that deity before you begin. To use myself as an example again, when I began my initial dedication to the Morrignae I clearly stated why I was doing it and what my ultimate goal was, as well as why I had chosen to go to Her/Them for that purpose.

Celtic Healing Deities

The following section is based on the hand-out from my class on Celtic healing deities from the Changing Times, Changing Worlds convention of 2011. It offers an overview of a selection of different Celtic Gods associated with healing, their basic folklore, and suggestions for offerings:

Brighid

Also known as Brigit, Bríd, Brig, Bric, Bride, Brigantia, Brigandu. A pan-Celtic Goddess, in Ireland she was a deity of healing, poetry and smithcraft, sometimes seen as a single deity and sometimes as three sister deities. Her name may mean 'exalted one'. Brighid is a Goddess associated especially with childbirth and fertility, and any healing relating to issues around those topics, but she is often called in folk charms for any type of healing at all, from toothaches to blood in urine. Brighid was said to possess two great oxen who would cry out during periods of pillaging, as well as a boar who was called 'king of the swine'; she was also strongly associated with sheep. As a patroness of farm animals she is often called on for healing animals, something that can be very useful in modern times. Brighid has a special healing well and site at Kildare and is associated with water that has healing powers, as well as a special talisman called a brat Bhride, which is a small piece of cloth left out on Imbolc Eve to be blessed by the Goddess/saint . This would then have healing properties throughout the year. Offerings to Brighid often include milk, butter, cheese, and bread, and in some cases chickens. Her special bird is the oystercatcher, which in Scottish is named Bridein, Bride's bird, and Gille Bride, paige of Bride. The linnet is also special to the Goddess and is named bigein Bride, little bird of Bride. Brighid's flower is the dandelion.

Airmed

Also known as Airmid, Airmeith and Airmedh, she is the daughter of the healing God Dian Cecht and sister of Miach. She is an Irish Goddess associated with herbal healing. In one version of the story of the healing of King Nuada by Miach, after Miach died Airmed found healing herbs growing from his grave and harvested them; she laid all the herbs out on her cloak and organized them to preserve the knowledge of their properties. Some sources say the herbs numbered 365, with one for each of his sinews and joints, and one for every possible bodily ailment. Many people today associate her especially with herbal healing. I have often used a mortar and pestle to represent her on my altar. She is also associated with the cloak or mantle, called a brat in Irish.

Miach

Miach is the Irish God associated with restoring the lost limb of the God Nuada and healing physical injuries up to those that are immediately fatal. He is the son of Dian Cecht and brother of Airmed. In some versions of the story of his healing of King Nuada, his father was so jealous of his healing powers that he dealt him four blows, the first three Miach healed but the fourth killed him; after this every healing herb in the world grew up from his grave and Airmed was organizing them when Dian Cecht scattered them (in other versions Miach is not killed). This is a reflection of the belief that the plants that grow on a person's grave hold some of their spirit, and so what grew from the grave of the healing God were all the healing plants in the world. Of course being a God his death was not permanent, but may have served the purpose of giving such plants to the world, in my opinion. Some people in a modern context associate Miach with surgical healing and reconstructive surgery.

Dian Cecht

Also spelled Dian Céacht, this Irish God is associated with physicians, healing, and restoring the body. Dian Cecht was considered the supreme physician of the Gods and possessed a well or cauldron into which the wounded could be placed and from which they would emerge restored. His name may mean 'swift traveler' and he is called 'the healing sage of Ireland' and 'God of health'. He is the father of two other Irish healing deities, Miach and Airmed, and in the mythological cycle is referred to as having three brothers who are also healers. Not only is he a God of active healing, he is also a God of the knowledge of healing arts and of healing magic. He is known as a superlative healer of any method. He possessed a magical cauldron or well that could heal any injury; some say he created his great healing well by placing one of every healing herb into it, and in mythology he is known to heal grievous wounds and cure plagues in the guise of dragons. The cauldron or well could be used as his symbol, perhaps with herbs in it.

Nodens

Also known in Wales as Nudd, or Llud Llaw Eirent (Llud the silver handed), he is sometimes equated to the Irish Nuada, and on the continent as Noadatus. Nodens is a pan-Celtic deity who the Romans synchronized with Mars, sometimes Silvanus, and in one case Neptune. His name may mean 'Cloud Maker' or 'Spirit of Water'. A God of healing, he had a shrine in Gloucestershire where votive offerings were made of bronze objects representing the area of the body the person needed to be healed, particularly limbs and eyes. He is especially associated with amputees because he was believed to have lost an arm in battle, which was later replaced with a silver one, hence the epithet 'silver hand'. His companion is a dog who can heal wounds by licking them. Besides dogs, he is particularly associated with salmon and trout, which may make good offerings to him.

Sulis

Also known as Sul, Sulei, and Sulla, she is syncretized with Minerva. Inscriptions at one of her sacred sites, the hot springs at Bath, imply that she may be a triple Goddess, referred to as the Sulevi. Her/their worship has been found from Switzerland to Britain and is always associated with hot springs. Sulis is associated with healing diseases and with childbirth. Coins and votive offerings were left on her shrines and in the water, generally after being purposefully damaged.

Belenus

Another pan-Celtic God, he is variously known as Bíle (to the Irish), Bellinus (in Britain), Belen (Welsh), and also Belenos, and Bel. His name likely means 'the shining God' and he is associated with the sun and sacred fire and syncretized with Apollo. Some authors think his healing associations may relate to his solar connection. He had temple sites in many parts of the Celtic world, but a significant one is in Burgundy where people would travel seeking cures for illnesses. Clay horses were left as offerings there to the God, indicating that horses may have been one of his sacred animals. In a modern setting Belenus may be called on especially for illnesses, and I think, for issues that the sun is a good treatment for, such as seasonal affective disorder. Images of horses could be offered to him as could written prayers.

References:

O hÓgain, D., (2006). The Lore of Ireland Carmichael, A., (1900). Carmina Gadelica, volume 1

Monaghan, P., (2004). Encyclopedia of Celtic Mythology and Folklore

O hOgáin, D., (1991). Myth, Legend, and Romance: an Encyclopedia of the Irish Folk Tradition

Green, M., (1992). Dictionary of Celtic Myth and Legend

Brighid

> *Three renovators of the world: the womb of woman, a cow's udder, a smith's moulding-block.*
> Traditional Irish Triad

One of the most popular Irish Goddesses in modern times is Brighid, also called Brigit, Bríd, Brig, Bric, Bride, Brigantia, Brigandu. A pan-Celtic Goddess, in Ireland she was a deity of healing, fertility, poetry and smithcraft, sometimes seen as a single deity and sometimes as three sister deities. O hOgáin says that Brighid, whose name probably means 'Exalted One', is a protector and inspirer of poets, as well as being connected to agricultural fertility. The 9th century glossaries say that 'among all the Irish a Goddess used to be called a Brigit' (O hOgáin, the Lore of Ireland). Of course most if not all Irish deity names are actually titles or epithets so it's hard to judge how meaningful that was in the pagan period, but it does add to the confusion about who exactly Brighid was and is from a pagan perspective. The information we have relating to Brighid comes from the traditional mythology including the Cath Maige Tuired and Lebor Gabála Érenn as well as mythology of the Christian saint of the same name who many believe is a continuation of the Goddess. Modern beliefs and practices surrounding Brighid are an amalgam of older pagan sources and newer Christian ones. Much of this is due to the logical assumption that many of the beliefs and practices surrounding the saint reflect older pre-Christian beliefs originally attached to the Goddess.

Finding anything clear-cut in Irish myth is difficult and this is true of trying to sort out Brighid's genealogy. In many cases Brighid's mother is not listed, she is simply called the daughter of the Dagda (or daughters of the Dagda as the case may be). Now what gets tricky is that in some medieval sources she is given as the mother of the three Gods of Danu, which is where some people come to think that she may be the same deity as Danu, although it is impossible to know with certainty if this is so, or only a medieval attempt to reconcile the pagan mythology into a more cohesive system. In mythology she was married to the Fomorian Bres and bore him a son Ruadan; in some stories she also had three sons with Tuireann named Brian, Iachar, and Iucharba, although this may result from confusion between her and Danu/Danand. She is viewed as the sister of Angus mac Og, which plays an important role in some of the recent stories surrounding Imbolc, Brighid's special holiday.

Imbolc is a holy day dedicated to the Goddess Brighid and is celebrated on February 1st or 2nd, although Carmichael mentions an older date as well of February 13th. The Gadelica mentions several traditions relating to this holiday. I've write in depth about Imbolc in a later chapter so I won't repeat everything here, but in brief it is a holiday specially dedicated to Brighid in both Ireland and Scotland. There are some modern stories that connect Brighid and the Cailleach at Imbolc; some people say that Imbolc is the day that the Cailleach Bhur releases Brighid who has been held prisoner all winter, while others say that Angus rescues his sister. Still another version says that Brighid and the Cailleach are the same deity, and that at Samhain Brighid becomes the Cailleach while at Imbolc she drinks from a sacred spring that turns her back into Brighid. Although the ideas connecting Brighid and the Cailleach are entirely modern, dating no further back than the 20th century, they have become increasingly popular among neopagans.

Brighid was said to have two oxen and a pig who would cry out 'after rapine had been committed in Ireland', which O hOgáin says relates her to domestic animals. He also sees her as a mother Goddess; the saint is referred to as the foster mother of Christ and this may well reflect an older feeling that Brighid was motherly to all those who prayed to her or honored her. Historian Peter Berresford Ellis also connects her to healing, fertility, smithcraft and poetry and mentions that she and Danu may be equivalents. Brighid has many strong associations to healing, fertility and healing of livestock, and also to protection and blessing in folk magic charms as can be seen in the Carmina Gadelica material. Brighid has a special healing well and site at Kildare and is associated with water that has healing powers, as well as a special talisman called a brat Bhride (Brigid's mantle or cloak), which is a small piece of cloth left out on Imbolc Eve to be blessed by the Goddess/saint, which would then have healing properties throughout the year. Personally I've always also associated Brighid with grief, mourning, and children because of an incident in the Cath Maige Tuired where her son Ruadan is killed and she is said to be the first to ever grieve and keen (caoine) in Ireland.

Offerings to Brighid often could include milk, butter, cheese, and bread, and in some cases chickens. For a modern practitioner these would all still be viable options and reflect Brighid's connection to agriculture and dairy products. According to Carmichael, her special bird is the oystercatcher, which in Scottish is named Bridein, Bride's bird, and Gille Bride, paige of Bride. The linnet is also special to the Goddess and is named bigein Bride, little bird of Bride. Brighid's flower is said to be the dandelion, and I have been told that the rowan tree was also particularly associated with her.

I am including my own version of a popular prayer to Brighid, the Genealogy of Brighid; this is the version from my book By Land, Sea and Sky.

Genealogy of Brighid (pagan version)

The genealogy of the holy Goddess Brighid,
Radiant flame of gold, noble mother of Ruadan,
Brighid, the daughter of an Daghda the Good God,
Every day and every night
That I say the genealogy of Brighid,
I shall not be killed, I shall not be harried,
I shall not be jailed , I shall not be wounded,
Nor shall my Gods leave me.

No fire, no sun, no moon shall burn me,
No lake, no water, nor sea shall drown mc,
No arrow of fairy nor dart of Fey shall wound me,
I am under the protection of the Gods of life,
And my gentle foster-mother is my beloved Brighid.

Modified based on material from volume 1 of the Carmina Gadelica by A. Carmichael, 1900.

References:

http://www.ucc.ie/celt/online/T103006.html
O hOgáin, D., (2006). The Lore of Ireland
Carmichael, A., (1900). Carmina Gadelica, volumes 1 and 2
Green, M., (1992). Dictionary of Celtic Myth and Legend
Macalister, R., (1941). Lebor Gabála Érenn. Part IV., Irish Texts Society, Dublin
http://brigitssparklingflame.blogspot.com/2009/04/more-than-winters-crone-cailleach-in.html

Flidais Foltchaion

Flidais is one of the more enigmatic and intriguing of the Irish deities. References to her in mythology are few and lack detail, yet there seems to be something deep and compelling about her. There is some debate about whether she is a historic deity or a literary creation of the later period, although it may be that her shifting character reflects euhumerization of the Goddess into a human literary character, rather than a purely literary creation.

Her name may mean 'wet one' and she is especially associated with milk and milking; her epithet is foltchaoin 'soft haired' (O hOgáin, 2006). Her husband was Adammair in one source and her son Nia Segamain (Leahy, 1906). In the Lebor Gabála Érenn her children are listed as Arden, Be Chuille, Dinand, and Be Teite and the Metrical Dindeshenchas list her as the mother of Fand (Macalister, 1941; Gwynne, 1906). In the Driving of the Cattle of Flidais she appears as a mortal character, the lover of Fergus mac Rog and wife of Ailill Finn (Leabor na h-Uidre, nd).

In the Lebor Gabála Érenn Flidais is said to be the owner of magical cattle, and two of her children, Be Chuille and Dinand, are referred to as 'she-farmers' connecting them to the produce of the earth, with another, Nia Segamain, mentioned in relation to her cattle (Macalister, 1941; Leahy, 1906). She was said to also have a herd of deer that gave milk like cows, and her herd was made up of both deer and cows (Keating, 1857). Monaghan suggests that her name means 'doe' and sees parallels between Flidias and continental Goddesses like Arto, Artemis, and Diana (Monaghan, 2004). She is associated with both domestic cattle and deer, and all animals are said to be her 'cattle' (O hOgáin, 2006). During the Tain Bo Cuiligne she supplied milk from her herd once a week that fed the entire army of Connacht, and in the Driving of the Herd of Flidais she was said to have one cow that could feed 300 men from one milking (Leabar na h-Uidre, nd). In this story as well we learn of Flidais's sexual prowess as she alone could satisfy her lover Fergus; without her it would take seven women to do the same (O hOgáin, 2006).

Modern Celtic pagans often associate Flidais with the woodlands and with wild animals, although in mythology she is equally connected to domestic animals. Deer and cattle are her special animals in mythology and could be used to represent her; offerings of milk would seem to be appropriate. Her nature in mythology seems to be both motherly, with her many children and connection to milk and milking, and also sensual in her role as the lover of Fergus. She also is clearly a deity of abundance and sustenance, who provides for all who rely on her. She has strong associations with sexuality that give an added depth to her nature; she is both domestic and wild, maternal and sexual.

There is at least one reference to Flidais as a healer; in the Driving of the Herd of Flidais it is said that she tended to and healed the men wounded in battle (Leabhar na h-Uidre, nd). Interestingly this may relate to a more modern folk charm against poison that calls on 'Fleithas', a name similar to the modern Irish for Flidias – Fliodhais. This charm refers to the hounds of Fliethas, as well as the three daughters of Fleithas (Wilde, 1991). These are possibly connections to the Irish Goddess Flidais and Fleithas and the healing charm can easily be modified to call on her. Below I am including the version I use from Lady Wilde's book Irish Cures, Mystic Charms & Superstitions with the possible modifications in parenthesis.

A Very Ancient Charm against Wounds or Poisons

The poison of a serpent, the venom of the dog,
The sharpness of spear, does not do well in man.
The blood of one dog, the blood of many dogs,
The blood of the hound of Fliethas (Flidais) – these I invoke.
It is not a wart to which my spittle is applied.
I strike disease; I strike wounds.
I strike the disease of the dog that bites,
Of the thorn that wounds
Of the iron that strikes.
I invoke the three daughters of Fleithas (Flidais)
Against the serpent
Benediction on this body to be healed;
Benediction on the spittle;
Benediction on him who casts out disease.

References:

Keating, G., (1857). Foras Feasa ar Éirinn

Leabhar na h-Uidre (nd) Retrieved from http://www. maryjone s.us/ctexts/flidais.html

O hOgáin, (2006). The Lore of Ireland

MacAlister. R. (1941). Lebor Gabála Érenn

Leahy, A., (1906). Heroic Romances of Ireland

Gwynne E., (1906). The Metrical Dindshenchas

Monaghan (2004). Encyclopedia of Celtic Myth and Folklore

Wilde (1991). Irish Cures, Mystic Charms & Superstitions

Macha, Goddess of Battle and Sovereignty

Macha is a Goddess of the Tuatha Dé Danann who appears in multiple places in mythology; while she is mentioned in various Irish myths she appears to have been a Goddess of Ulster and Northern Ireland in particular. Macha is the sister of Badhbh and Anand or Anu; these three are listed as three daughters of Ernmas and are often said to be the three aspects of the Morrigan, although sometimes Nemain is listed as an alternate to Anand/Anu. O'Mulconry's glossary calls her 'machæ .i. badb no asi an tres morrigan', meaning Macha, a scald-crow, or the third Morrigan, which confirms her connection to the Morrigan (Stokes, 1898).

In her first mythic appearance she is the wife of Nemed, of the third race to settle Ireland, and in this tale she 'dies', clearing the plains of Ireland for farming. In alternate versions, her husband cleared the land and she died there so he named it for her. In at least one version she has a vision of the future Cattle Raid of Cooley and her heart breaks at the grief that will come from that, killing her. In all these cases she is linked to the earth and its produce; it is also possible that her name 'Macha' may mean plain or field, although in Old Irish the word is related to both fields and to milk cattle.

She appears in the epic myth cycle the Lebor Gabála Érenn, which provides us with some of the strongest evidence about her character and powers. In volume IV of the Lebor translation by R. A. S. Macalister, the translator says, 'Delbaeth... has three daughters, the famous war-furies Badb, Macha, and Mórrígu, the latter sometimes called Anand or Danand.' (Macalister, 1941). According to the Lebor Gabála Érenn, Macha is the wife of King Nuada and it is said that she is killed with Nuada in battle. It seems most likely though that this Macha and the later appearances of Macha are all referring to the same individual. Macalister also says:

> *Macha, one of the Badb sisterhood, has a certain individuality of her own, and enjoyed a special cult, probably centered at Armagh (Ard Macha), to which she bequeathed her name. Her intrusion into the Badb sisterhood may be a subsequent development, for the genealogies before us seem to suggest an earlier tradition in which Badb and the variously named third member of the group formed a dyad.*
> (Macalister, 1941).

This further strengthens her connection to the Morrigan, but also indicates a separateness that is important to note. The information from the Lebor Gabála Érenn also indicates that Macha entered the actual battle alongside the warriors of the Tuatha Dé Danann as well as indicating her place alongside her sisters directing battle magics at the enemy. In the Banshenchus she is listed as one of the Tuatha Dé Danann's magic workers, and it tells us that in the first battle of Mag Tuired she acts with the other two Morrigans to use magic against the enemy, specifically by sending rain, fog, and showers of blood and fire upon the opposing army. The second battle of Mag Tuired lists the three Morrigans as ban-draoithe, or Druids (Gray, 1983). Macha is a master of battle in both a physical and magical way, connecting her to warriors and to magic users.

Next she appears as a fairy woman who moves in uninvited to the home of the peasant Crunnchu, where she assumes the role of his wife and becomes pregnant by him. Eventually he goes to a festival held by the king and after hearing the king brag about the speed of his racing horses begins to brag about Macha's speed at racing, even though she has warned him not to tell anyone about her presence. Irate at this boasting by the peasant the king immediately demands that Macha be brought before him in order to race his horses or Crunnchu will be killed. Macha is brought before the king and his court but begs that the race be delayed as she has gone into labor; the king and nobles callously force her to race anyone, ignoring her pleas. The Goddess wins the race, easily outpacing the horses, but collapses just past the finish line and gives birth to twins. As she delivers her children she curses the men of Ulster for nine times nine generations, that they will feel the pain of a woman in labor for nine days when in the hour of their greatest need. In some versions of the story she dies while others have her returning to the Otherworld. The places that these events occurred carry her name to this day, Emain Macha, and for many centuries assemblies were held there, particularly on Lughnasa. It is from this story that her associations with horses, childbirth, pregnancy, justice, and, again, the produce of the earth – by marrying a peasant – are seen.

In the next story we see her connection to sexuality, sovereignty, and battle. She is Macha Mog Ruadh, Macha Red-Hair, daughter of one of three kings who share the kingship of Ireland, each ruling for seven years in turn. When her father dies, Macha steps up to rule, but is challenged by the other two kings who do not want to co-rule with a woman. She battles them and wins, and when her seven years are up she refuses to turn leadership over to the others since she is Queen not by blood but through victory in battle. One of the two kings dies, leaving five sons who would challenge her, so she goes to them in the appearance of a crone or leper and seduces them one by one, tying them up afterwards and thereby defeating them and enslaving them. Finally she marries the last of the original three kings, Cimbaeth.

Traditionally the severed heads of enemy warriors were called 'Macha's acorn crop', another sign that she was a warrior Goddess. My personal view is that in each story when she 'dies' she is actually just returning to the Otherworld from whence she came, having accomplished what she intended in our world. I have found her to be a fiercely loving Goddess, who is protective of those she calls her own – with a very strong 'mother' energy – while at the same time she can be very no-nonsense and unbending as well. She always appears to me as a red-haired warrior woman wearing a cloak of black feathers and riding or walking next to a black or white horse, sometimes both. To me she is a Goddess of the sovereignty of the land, a protector of the weak, and Goddess of women and women's issues, especially pregnancy and childbirth – which is definitely a form of battle.

References:

Rolleston, T., (n.d.) Myths and Legends of the Celtic Race. Retrieved from http://www.sacred-texts.com/neu/celt/mlcr

/mlcr05.htm
Gray, E. (1983). Cath Maige Tuired. Published by the Irish Texts Society.
Macalister, R. (1941). Lebor Gabála Érenn, volume IV. Published by the Irish Texts Society
Stokes, W. (1898). O'Mulconry's Glossary
Personal gnosis

Nuada Argatlamh

Nuada was the king of the Tuatha Dé Danann when they first came to Ireland; in the Lebor Gabála Érenn it is said that he ruled for seven years before the Tuatha de Danann came to Ireland, was displaced when he lost an arm in battle, and then ruled a further 20 years after being healed (Macalister, 1941). Nuada was the son of Echtach, and had four sons, Tadg, Caither, Cucharn, and Etaram the poet, as well as a daughter, Echtge; no mother is mentioned (Gray, 1983). He is said in some sources to be married to Macha, one of the three Morrignae, and he possessed one of the four treasures brought to Ireland by the Tuatha Dé Danann, a sword which once unsheathed no enemy could escape and no wound from it could be healed (Berresford Ellis, 1987; O hOgáin, 2006; Jones, 2012). O hOgáin suggests that his name may mean 'catcher' and theorizes that Nuada is the same deity as Nechtan and Elcmar (O hOgáin, 2006). He suggests this based on another name for Nuada being Nuada Necht, which O hOgáin believes is the earlier form of Nechtan; by this association Nuada would have been the original owner of Brugh na Boyne and would also possess the source of the Boyne, the well of Nechtan. Although difficult to prove with certainty this would reflect the strong connection to water seen in the related British deity, Nodens.[2] Other sources also suggest Nuada as being the same deity as Nechtan and Elcmar, making him the husband of Boand who is cuckolded by the Dagda and then tricked out of possession of the Brugh na Boyne by Boand and Dagda's son from the affair,

Angus (Monaghan, 2004). Based on this idea it would appear that after losing the Brugh to Angus Nuada moved to Sidhe Chleitigh, although alternate stories later claim his home to be sidhe Almhu or Slievenamon (Green, 1992; Monaghan, 2004; O hOgáin, 2006).

Nuada's most well known epithet is Airgetlamh, silver hand or arm. His name also appears as Nuadha, Nuadae, Nuadai, and Nuodai, with alternate spellings of his epithet as Aircetlaum (Gray, 1983). In the story of the Cath Maige Tuired Nuada was said to have lost his arm in battle, after which Dian Cecht, with the help of the smith Credne, fashioned him a new arm of silver that looked and moved just as a real arm would (Macalister, 1941). According to a note by Gray in the Index to Persons of the Cath Maige Tuired there is a story where Nuada's severed arm is carried off after the battle by a hawk (Gray, 1983). Because of this disfigurement Nuada was forced to relinquish his kingship, for the law of the Tuatha Dé Danann stated that only an unblemished king could rule (Monaghan, 2004; Macalister, 1941). O hOgáin suggests, in his book The Lore of Ireland, that the original story of the loss of Nuada's arm may have actually involved an accident with his own sword, or even an intentional sacrifice, and that there may have been some connection to healing waters or even that his lost arm may have been symbolic of a river (O hOgáin, 2006). During the medieval period the story was expanded to include more details; it was his right arm that was lost in battle with the Fir Bolg warrior Streang (O hOgáin, 2006; Gray, 1983). Nuada was carried from the field only to return the next day with the request that Streang tie his own right arm to ensure fair combat – when Streang refused the other Tuatha Dé Danann offered a province of land to keep Nuada from risking his life in an unequal fight (Gray, 1983; O hOgáin, 2006). At this point Bres became king, but after seven years Dian Cecht fashioned the silver arm, then his son Miach, possibly along with Ormiach, replaced it with an arm of flesh and Nuada took back the kingship, beginning the second battle of Maige Tuired (Macalister, 1941; Monaghan, 2004; O hOgáin, 2006). During the second battle Nuada gives the kingship to Lugh, who organizes the battle and fights the fearsome Fomorian Balor, who is Lugh's grandfather (Green, 1992). By some accounts Nuada ruled for 20 years after being healed, while others state that he and Macha died together in the second battle of Maige Tuired at the hand of Balar the Fomorian king (Gray, 1983; Macalister, 1941).

Nuada is a complex deity who can be seen as a God of battle, war, and also justice (Gray, 1983). Some sources also connect him to hunting (Jones, 2012). If weight is given to the parallels between Nuada and Nodens and to the possible connections to Nechtan and Elcmar then he could also be seen as a God of healing and of the water, particularly rivers. The sword would be one of his symbols, as he possessed the sword that was one of the four treasures, and hawks may be associated with him. I personally have experienced the hawk as a symbol and messenger of Nuada, long before finding out the version of the story that connected him to the bird through the loss of his arm. Dogs and salmon/trout may also be associated with him, again if the link with Nodens and the Boyne is accepted. As Nechtan he would be connected to salmon through the salmon of knowledge that lived at the source of the river Boyne. Appropriate offerings would seem to be fish, and I have offered beer and Guinness.

Green suggests that Nuada's name may mean 'cloud-maker' and suggests that his counterparts in other cultures include Nodens, Nudd/Ludd, and possibly the Germanic Tyr (Green, 1992). The arguments put forth to connect the deities are reasonably sound, relying on the shared reconstructed Indo-European roots of 'noudont' or 'noudent', which means 'to catch' and proto-Indo-European root 'neu-d', which means 'to acquire' or 'to utilize' (Nodens, 2012). However, as with anything involving reconstructed language, it is still only theoretical.

There also seems to be a fairly strong mythological connection between these deities, particularly around the loss of an arm and replacement of the limb with one of silver. As I have researched this I have decided for myself that I am comfortable with hÓgain's logic in connecting Nuada with Nechtan and Elcmar, and also the likely pan-Celtic parallels between Nuada and Nodens, Nudd/Ludd, and Noadatus. I am least comfortable with the connection to the Germanic God Tyr, although I can see the argument for an ancient root deity shared in common. Readers are welcome to draw their own conclusions.

References:

Berresford Ellis, P., (1987). Dictionary of Irish Mythology

Green, M., (1992). Dictionary of Celtic Myth and Legend

Monaghan, P., (2004). Encyclopedia of Celtic Mythology and Folklore

O hOgáin, D., (2006). the Lore of Ireland

Macalister, R., (1941). Lebor Gabála Érenn

Gray, E., (1983). Cath Maige Tuired

Evans, D., (2011). http://www.celtnet.org.uk/Gods_n/nudd.html

Jones, M., (2012). Nodens http://www.maryjones.us/jce/nodens.html

Nodens (2012). Websters Online Dictionary. http://www.websters-online-dictionary.org/definitions/Nodens

Áine

It's an interesting thing in Irish mythology and folklore that the Gods were reduced not into human characters, by and large, but into fairies. So it is with Áine of Cnoc Áine in county Kerry who is believed to have been a Goddess originally but is held to be a Lady of the Sí now with the fairy hill of Knockainy being her special place. Now my own view is that it doesn't really matter whether a being is a God in every story or sometimes appears as a fairy, as I see beings as on a scale of power where a powerful enough fairy and a God within a sí are effectively the same. It's sort of a potato/pah-tah-to situation where the label is incidental to the actual being.

Like most Irish deities, Áine has a complex and sometimes contradictory mythology. She is said in some sources to be the daughter of Manannan Mac Lir and in others to be the daughter of Manannan's foster son Eogabail, a Druid of the Tuatha Dé Danann (Berresford Ellis, 1987). No mother is listed for her. Some sources say that her sister is Finnen, whose name means white (Monaghan, 2004). Her name likely means 'brightness' or 'splendor' and she is often associated with the sun (O hÓgain, 2006; Monaghan, 2004). In fact not far from her hill of Cnoc Áine is another hill, Cnoc Gréine, associated with the Goddess Grian (literally 'Sun') who is also reputed be a fairy queen; MacKillop suggests the two Goddesses might represent the summer and winter suns respectively and some sources list them as sisters (MacKillop, 1998; Monaghan, 2004).

There is some confusion in modern mythology where Áine is seen as an aspect of Anu or the Morrigan, but Berresford Ellis sees this connection as unlikely (Berresford Ellis, 1987). Interestingly Grian is similarly seen as a possible aspect of Macha, probably due to a reference to Macha in the Metrical Dindesenchas that gives an epithet of Grian to her. While I disagree with these associations, I admit that I find it fascinating that Áine and Grian are strongly associated with each other and a possible division of the year, and each is also associated with the Morrigan and Macha respectively. There is also a trend for describing Áine as a moon Goddess, although there is nothing in myth or folklore to support that.

In much of her later folklore Áine is reputed to have love affairs with mortals and several Irish families claim descent from her. The most well known of these human descendants is the third Earl of Desmond, Gearoid Iarla. It is said by some that Gearoid did not die but was taken into Loch Guirr and would return one day (Berresford Ellis, 1987). Other tales say that he lives still within the lake and can be seen riding beneath the water on a white fairy horse, while still other stories claim that Áine turned him into a goose on the shore of the lake (Berresford Ellis, 1987). She was also said to have been raped by the king Aillil Olom, on Samhain, who stories say she either bit an ear off of or she killed in punishment (Monaghan, 2004; Berresford Ellis, 1987; O hÓgain, 2006). The child of this union was Eogan whose line went on to claim rulership of the land through their descent from the Goddess (Monaghan, 2004).

Áine is associated with fertility, agriculture, sovereignty, and the sun, as well as love (Berresford Ellis, 1987; Monaghan, 2004). She is associated especially with red mares, with some people claiming she could assume this form (MacKillop, 1998; Monaghan, 2004). She may also be associated more generally with horses and possibly with geese and sheep as they appear in her folklore. The hill of Cnoc Áine is one of the most well known places associated with her, said to have been named after her during the settling of Ireland when she used magic to help her father win the area (O hÓgain, 2006). Midsummer was her special holy day and up until the 19th century people continued to celebrate her on the eve of Midsummer with a procession around the hill, carrying torches of burning straw in honor of Áine of the Wisps (Berresford Ellis, 1987). Áine is also sometimes called Áine Chlair, a word that may relate to wisps or may be an old name for the Kerry or Limerick area (Monaghan, 2004; O hÓgain, 2006). On midsummer clumps of straw would be lit on her hill and then scattered through the cultivated fields and cows to propitiate Áine's blessing (O hÓgain, 2006). In county Louth there is a place called Dun Áine where people believe that the weekend after Lughnasa belongs to Áine, and in some folklore she is said to be the consort of Crom Cruach during the three days of Lughnasa (O hÓgain, 2006; MacNeill, 1962). Additionally there is another hill called Cnoc Áine in county Derry, and a third in Donegal (O hÓgain, 2006). In Ulster there is a well called Tobar Áine that bears her name.

Whether a Goddess or fairy queen Áine has been much loved, even up until fairly recently. Her mythology is convoluted, but fascinating, and any who feel the need or desire to honor a solar Goddess within an Irish framework would do well to learn more about Áine. I have honored her at midsummer for many years, and am glad I do. As is said, she is 'the best hearted woman who ever lived' (O hÓgain, 2006).

References:

Berresford Ellis, P., (1987). A Dictionary of Irish Mythology

O hÓgain, D., (2006). The Lore of Ireland

Monaghan, P., (2004). The Encyclopedia of Celtic Mythology and Folklore

MacKillop, J., (1998). A Dictionary of Celtic Mythology

MacNeill, M., (1962). Festival of Lughnasa

Manannán mac Lir

One of the deities that can be found in the mythology of several different Celtic nations is Manannán; called Manannán mac Lir (son of the sea) in Ireland, and Manawydan to the Welsh. His home was said to be the Isle of Man, called Manaw in Welsh and Manu in Irish; Manannán's name clearly derives from this and since this name for the island is a later development O hÓgain posits that Manannán himself and his mythology are later developments as well, likely dating to no earlier that the 3rd century CE (O hÓgain, 2006). The Irish initially borrowed the name from the Welsh, but then added the title 'mac Lir', which was then borrowed into the Welsh as 'map Llyr' (O hÓgain, 2006). This demonstrates the composite nature of Manannán that has developed over time as the cultures shared mythology back and forth. To the Manx he was the first king of the Island of Man, and stories locate his grave there, as well as tell of how he would walk among the Manx fishermen as they repaired their nets (Monaghan, 2004).

Manannán's appearance is described as being that of a handsome warrior (Berresford Ellis, 1987). Manannán's wife is Fand, a peerless beauty who at one point had an affair with Cu Chulain, until Manannán used his magic to make Cu Chulain forget about her and return to his own wife, Emer. It is said that Manannán traveled to the mortal world to father Mongán, a prince and hero, and under the name of Oirbsiu he may have fathered the Conmhaicne sept of Leinster (O hÓgain, 2006). There are many stories about his various sons and daughters, who are usually treated as minor characters (O hÓgain, 2006). One of his more well known children is Áine, although some sources list her as his wife.

Manannán was originally said to live on the Isle of Man, a place which was seen as near mythical in Irish stories; later his home shifted fully into the Otherworld, to Eamhain (O hÓgain, 2006). The Irish described Eamhain in rich detail as a sacred place, an island held up by four silver legs or pillars, on which grew magical apples which gave the island the full name of Eamhain Abhlach, Eamhain of the Apples (O hÓgain, 2006). Other names for his domain include Mag Meall (the pleasant plain) and Tír Tairngire (the land of promise) (O hÓgain, 2006). Each of these names and associations reflect the connection between Manannán's realm and the Otherworld.

To the Welsh, Manannán – or more properly Manawydan – was a skilled craftsman and trickster deity (O hÓgain, 2006). To the Irish, however, he was seen as the lord of the waves, to whom the ocean was like a field of solid land, as well as a master magician and God who could control the weather (O hÓgain, 2006). The fish are said to be his livestock, compared to cows and sheep, and the waves themselves are called his horses; his most special horse is Enbharr, 'water foam', who could run over sea as if it were solid land (O hÓgain, 2006). In the story of his meeting with King Cormac mac Art he is described as carrying a golden apple branch that rang with sweet music that could sooth people to sleep or heal the ill and wounded (O hÓgain, 2006). Some sources consider him a shapeshifter, and his magical powers were numerous; he could travel faster than the wind could blow in his magical boat, he could create realistic illusions, and he had a cloak of forgetfulness that would take the memory from a person (Monaghan, 2004). It was this cloak that he used to cause Cu Chulain to forget Fand in the story of the Only Jealousy of Emer.

In Irish mythology, although he was not counted among the People of Danu in stories until the 10th century, it is Manannán who advises the Tuatha Dé Danann to take up residence in the sidhe, and he who assigned each new home (O hÓgain, 2006). Additionally, he gives three gifts to the Tuatha de; the féth fiadha, the feast of Goibhniu, and the pigs of Manannán (O hÓgain, 2006). The féth fiadha was either a spell or cloak that allowed the person to become invisible and travel unnoticed. The feast of Goibhniu was a magical feast that kept the Gods young and living. The pigs of Manannán were immortal swine that could be killed and would return to life. Some sources suggest it was these actions that earned him a place among the Tuatha Dé Danann. However, I believe that it is more likely that he fills a role as an outsider deity, not fully part of the People of Danu nor fully outside their ranks, but liminally placed. Even his realm, which is a land that is not part of the land, reflects this idea.

Manannán's nature is as mercurial as the sea. When visiting Elcmar at his sidhe he is paid great tribute with rushes laid out before him and a great feast prepared, yet despite the pleasant visit he dislikes Elcmar and acts against him later (O hÓgain, 2006). In the stories of the Fianna, Manannán is often helpful yet also appears at least once to stir strife and create trouble among the warriors (O hÓgain, 2006). This could reflect the knowledge of all sailors that the favor of the sea is fickle and quick to change, or perhaps Manannán's own liminal nature tends toward changeability.

In several sources rushes are mentioned as offerings for him, so it could be safely assumed that rushes were historically sacred to him (O hÓgain, 2006). The sea and waters were also strongly associated with him, and it said in the story of Oirbsiu that when he died a lake burst forth from his grave. He is also strongly associated with horses and apples. Many modern Druids see Manannán as the keeper of the gates between our world and the Otherworld and call on him to open the way between the worlds.

Living near the ocean I tend to feel his presence in the fog and mist, as well as sometimes in the ocean waves. I believe it is important when connecting to Manannán to remember the truly awesome power of the ocean and of water, both to nourish and to destroy; power that reflects and is reflected by Manannán's own personality and actions in mythology. The same ocean that feeds and comforts us can as easily kill us if we do not respect it; the river that gives us water to drink and a place to swim can rise up in a flood and destroy our homes. Manannán can bless us or harm us, and we would be wise to remember the true nature of his power as we honor him.

Reference:

Berresford Ellis, P., (1987). A Dictionary of Irish Mythology

Monaghan, P., (2004). The Encyclopedia of Celtic Myth and Folklore

O hÓgain, D., (2006). The Lore of Ireland

Artio, Germano-Celtic Bear Goddess

Sometimes the deities we feel drawn to worship are fairly well known in mythology or can easily be read about in secondary sources material, but other times we are drawn to deities that are obscure. This is the case with one of the main deities I honor, a Germano-Celtic Goddess named Artio; in practical terms it means that I have a scant few references to work with and must make up the difference with personal gnosis and experience. I have hesitated to write too much in the past about her because I knew that it would mean talking about personal practices that were developed through inspiration more than research, but it seems only fair now to offer what I know and my own experiences. Perhaps it will help others who feel drawn to or called by this particular obscure deity to feel more connected to her.

Artio is also called Dea Artio and Andarta, all names that relate to or directly mean 'bear' (Monaghan, 2004). One of the best known pieces of evidence relating to Artio is an engraved statue found near Berne, Switzerland. The statue depicts a seated female figure, generally thought to be the Goddess, holding a basket of fruit, facing a bear who is standing in front of a tree; an engraving on one side of the statue says: 'to the Goddess Artio' (Green, 1992). A second find with an inscription was found in Bollendorf, Germany, and other evidence was in France (Green, 1992; Monaghan, 2004). While the areas Artio has been found in could be considered Germanic, the name is Gallic, and she is generally described as either Germano-Celtic or Romano-Gaulish (I favor the former myself). Although the imagery of the statue is obscure and there is a lack of literary evidence, most agree that Artio was likely a Goddess of fertility and plenty, and possibly a patroness of hunters as well as protector of bears (Green, 1992; Markale, 1986). Some also theorize that she was a more general Goddess of the wilderness and wild things (Monaghan, 2004). Sources agree that she was also seen in the form of a bear, with Sjoestedt placing her in the category of zoomorphic Goddesses alongside Epona (Sjoestedt, 1949). It seems likely that the bear Goddess Artio was eventually replaced by a bear God Artaios who was synchretized by the Romans to Mercury (Markale, 1986).

My connection to Artio comes through my seidhr work. When I first seriously began to practice seidhr I decided I needed to find out who or what was willing to act as a guide and protector for me. I already had a close working relationship with my Fylgja and with certain plant and animal spirits, but I suspected that taking this sort of spiritual work in a new direction would involve new Powers, beyond Odin and Freya who were already involved. I undertook a spiritual journey and encountered a bear who was also a woman, simultaneously. She told me that she would be with me for any seidhr or spae work that I did and that her name was Artio. I had never heard that name before, but I knew that Art meant bear so I didn't think much of it. I was also told that when I did oracular spae work I should wear a bear skin instead of a veil. I assumed she was some sort of powerful spirit, and was happy that I had someone willing to be with me in this work.

By coincidence (or synchronicity) shortly after this experience I came across a fossilized cave bear tooth for sale and I bought it and made a necklace from it, which I have since worn whenever doing any seidhr or spae work. The bear fur was, suffice to say, much more difficult to find, but did come to me in due time and I use it as I was told to. I even recently had a dream where I 'won' a bear skull and was instructed to feed it by blooding it; I'm waiting to see if such a skull finds its way to me in the real world or not. I later found out that Artio was an actual historic Goddess, although there is nothing in the scant records to indicate a definite connection to any type of oracular or magical work associated with her. I don't know why I was surprised that I ended up contacting an obscure Germano-Celtic Goddess, since, in retrospect, that makes perfect sense as the sort of deity for me with my dual-trad ways. I can comfortably honor her in either a Celtic or Norse (Germanic) context, which is nice. This connection has always worked for me and I feel very protected by her in seidhr working and also very connected to the bear. Although I will say that my personal experiences with her show that she can be both tender and protective and also very intense.

I have encountered her in the Spiritworld and been dismembered, for example, but I have also been healed; I have had her in bear form charge at me roaring so that I was literally too terrified to move or even think, but she has also been very gentle with me. I have a small shrine for her with a collection of carved bear statues and the best image I could find of a Goddess and bear. I also honor her especially on the equinoxes. In the spring I celebrate the awakening of the bear on the spring equinox with a ritual for her that includes offerings of honey and bread. In September I celebrate the dreaming of the bear on the fall equinox with offerings of fresh fruit and vegetables. This is purely my own invention, although my kindred have adopted the practice along with me. We all practice seidhr together and have adopted Artio as a group, which seems to be working well.

Honoring Artio has forced me to trust my own intuition more and to be willing to follow my gut as I find ways to connect to a deity where there is very little existing historic information to rely on. I have also discovered a great deal about bears as I worked on learning about the animal most strongly connected to this deity. Bears are amazing animals, and I have found female bears particularly interesting; they are devoted mothers and excellent teachers, fierce and intelligent. Bears have several biological quirks, not only do they hibernate, but a female bear can delay pregnancy after fertilization through a process that scientists are still trying to understand. I encourage anyone drawn to Artio to begin studying bears as well (I've focused mostly on black bears because they are native to my region).

References:

Sjoestedt, M., (1949). Celtic Gods and Heroes

Markale, J., (1986). Women of the Celts

Green, M., (1992). Dictionary of Celtic Myth and Legend

Monaghan, P., (2004). Encyclopedia of Celtic Mythology and Folklore

Spirits of the Otherworld, Spirits of the Land

One thing that both the Irish and Norse culture share is a fairly similar view of Otherworldly spirits, often in modern times called fairies. Since honoring, connecting, and working with these spirits is, and always has been, the main aspect of my practice it probably isn't that surprising that I feel drawn to both systems of belief. My own views are based equally on study and experience, although talking about the latter is challenging for me. What I have found though is that many modern pagans and reconstructionists have vastly different views on this subject than I do, although I'm not entirely sure why. Where I see real beings that are powerful and intelligent, others talk about caricatures of elemental forces, simplified and minimal, or myths from the past that are treated as a thing of the past. Sometimes I wonder if many of the people talking about the spirits really even believe in them at all, or if it's just an intellectual exercise.

People talk about connecting to spirits of sacred places or wanting to go visit somewhere that has a reputation for certain spirits, when there are plenty of Otherwordly beings around us where we are. Even cities have their own spirits that abide in them. And when people do acknowledge the spirits where they live they do it in ways that often strike me as odd, although I am obviously only speaking my own opinion here. So this section is going to be mostly my opinions and views about the spirits of the land and of the Otherworld, and I will say up front that this is all very real to me. Before I knew the pagan Gods, before I had any religion to speak of, I knew the aos sidhe; that connection is the bedrock of my belief and my practice.

Firstly there is the assumption that to connect to local spirits we must understand the local beliefs about those spirits. Now on the one hand I will never argue against research and a better understanding of another cultures' views. But, honestly, I think this can get over-intellectualized; if you want to know the spirits of the area you live in (or your home) then get out there and make the effort to get to know them. Do it and let them get to know you, without getting caught up in what names to use or what offerings are traditional – that part should come organically over time. What matters is reaching out. Obviously in some cases they may just have no interest in you, or even feel antipathy, and if that happens respect it and leave them alone. But I digress. My point here is that what matters is making the effort. In my own experience I don't think any one type of spirit is limited to one culture or area, but rather that different cultures found their own names to describe the same type of spirit, just the same as animals and plants were named differently from one area and culture to another. Variations exist, to be sure, but not so dramatically that a person couldn't make an offering to the spirit of the local river even if they don't know its mythic history.

I realize this is a broad generalization, and will not be true of everyone – I certainly know people personally who are exceptions to what I'm about to say – but in general I have found that many pagans tend to take an oddly bifurcated approach to the denizens of the Otherworld, separating them into two groups (like the title of this section of the book) as if they really were separate, when the reality is much more simple and far more complicated. Being animists, most will acknowledge spirits of place and spirits of objects like trees and rivers, but it seems to be done in a superficial way, either imagined as vague feelings of awareness, or as primitive sentience, particularly when spirits of place are brought up. There is also an idea that these spirits exist only out in nature, and while it may be true that many prefer not to be near human habitations, for a variety of reasons, there are plenty enough that don't mind. Otherworldly beings are viewed anywhere from the stereotypical Victorian fairies to comical or mischievous to elemental forces, but again rarely seen with any real personality or depth. I can't even tell how many times I've heard or seen people referring to all beings of the Otherworld as if they were plant spirits or guardians of our natural world. As if anything with the aos sidhe was that simple or clear cut. I think what probably bothers me the most, personally, is that there is often an almost condescending attitude about the spirits, as if they require us to care for them, or conversely, as if they exist only to guide us. In my own worldview we do not rank above the spirits in the grand scheme of Power, rather we are at one end of the scale with the Gods at the other and the multitude of spirits in-between.

The traditional belief in both Irish and Icelandic cultures is that there are a wide array of spirit beings, and that these beings can bring luck or harm depending on their mood, inclination, and your actions. In Norse belief these beings can include everything from the dead to land spirits, from Alfar (elves) to trolls and other fairy-type beings. In the Irish culture, there is a similar view that the aos sidhe may include the dead, the taken, spirits of particular places, and an almost endless variety of beings, from pixies to the Alfar-like nobility. The beings of the Otherworld can grant luck and healing, or can torment people and bring illness or death. In Iceland even up to today this belief remains strong enough that roads and other construction are often done with the elves in mind, lest they be angered. In Ireland within the last ten years roads have been rerouted or redesigned to avoid tearing down or pulling up fairy trees, an act which is believed to curse the people responsible.

The coat of arms of Iceland features the image of four landvaettir, or land spirits, a dragon, bird, bull, and giant, who are believed to stand at the cardinal points and protect the island to this day. And here we can see the first difference between traditional belief and the common modern belief, because the land spirits (landvaettir) are not seen as vague consciousness at all but as physical spirits with form, awareness and intent. In the same way the fairies are seen as being dangerous to those who disturb them or destroy what belongs to them, not as harmless little creatures or as gentle guides for us. Fairies are not angelic beings, out for our greater good, but rather are independent sentient beings who may or may not be willing to help us, usually at a price.

Although it is true that dealing with the spirits is always a tricky thing, and often dangerous, it is also true that it can be beneficial and in many ways is, I think, necessary. Historically, cultures have always had someone who acts as an intercessory between human society and these beings, and so we still have them today, but it is not required to become a fairy a doctor or seidhr worker to respect and honor the spirits around us. One way to build a relationship with your local spirits is to leave regular offerings; generally milk, cream, or honey work well. I do understand that not everyone perceives Otherworldly beings and that for those who can't see or speak to spirits it really is an act of faith to connect to something that can't be verified by concrete evidence. But hasn't that always been the way of it? For every man or woman who sees them and for every story spread about interactions with them, there are hundreds more who never see them or even sense them in any way, yet still believe and incorporate honoring them into daily life. At a minimum, if offerings are more than you want to give, at least think of the Otherworldly beings around you – whether ghosts, spirits of place, or fairies – as you might your human neighbors. Be polite, be considerate, show respect.

References:

http://www.nytimes.com/2005/07/13/international/europe/13elves.html?_r=1

http://www.dw.de/dw/article/0,,2786922,00.html

http://www.sacred-texts.com/neu/yeats/twi/index.htm

http://www.sacred-texts.com/neu/celt/sce/index.htm

http://www.sacred-texts.com/neu/celt/ffcc/index.htm

Gundarsson, K., (2007). Elves, wights, and Trolls

http://www.sacred-texts.com/lcr/index.htm

Honoring the Good Neighbors: Modern Fairy Faith in America

The Good Neighbors comprise a huge aspect of my own personal practice and I feel like I really should discuss the subject here. Perhaps I am just feeling brave as I write this, as it is said that one should not discuss one's own personal experiences with the People of Peace.

First off I cannot emphasize enough that my view of the fairies is very different from most other modern pagans, at least in my own experience. I have what I call an 'old school' approach to them that is perfectly in line with what you'll find in Irish folklore and writing from 100 years ago by authors like Yeats and Wilde, but is generally at odds with the belief in modern paganism. For me the term 'fairy' is something of a catch-all that can describe any being that is not a human nor clearly categorized as a deity, angel, or the like. Fairies can be or appear as animals or as giants, as tiny people or as very human seeming. Fairy beings often seem mercurial to humans because they operate on an entirely different culture and etiquette system than we do. They can be cruel and vicious, or generous and kind. Some of them are helpful. Some are indifferent. And some of them think we make a very tasty meal indeed. And all of them take being insulted or disrespected very badly.

To quote the movie Labyrinth:

Sarah: *Ow! It bit me!*
Hoggle: *What'd you expect fairies to do?*
Sarah: *I thought they did nice things, like... like granting wishes.*
Hoggle: *Shows what you know, don't it?*

Pretty much like that. Except sometimes much more frightening. It always surprises me that people want to have close dealings with fairies, as it is a risky thing at best for most and if you study the Celtic Fairy Faith it becomes clear that most of the honoring was done to avoid mischief or as appeasement, not to draw them in. In fact many people avoid saying the word fairy or naming a specific type of fairy for fear of drawing their attention; instead a nickname is used that invokes a pleasant image, such as Mother's Blessing or the Gentry. Fairies can cause madness, can torment a person or animal, and can cause seemingly invisible injuries, called elfshot, which might manifest as sudden unexplainable pain or cramping in a leg or arm. Strokes were once even thought to be the result of elfshot.

Why would anyone choose to offer to them or deal with them? Well on the one hand some of them are capable of doing great harm and it's not a bad idea to be on their good side to avoid that, when possible. On the other they can bless a person with great luck or fortune, or even (as in the cases of the old Fairy Doctors) with knowledge of healing and magic. And for most pagans and magic workers it's probably a good idea to have some knowledge of the Fey and to be respectful, to maintain good relations as it were.

Me personally? I have been aware of them for so long that they are simply another part of my life, thanks to what the Irish call the second sight. I also have what can best be described as an ancestral connection in that area that shapes how I approach the subject. By the time I was old enough to start reading the written material that's out there, such as The Fairy Faith in Celtic Countries by W. Y. Evans-Wentz or Yeats' Celtic Twilight, I found that it was only reflecting my own experiences. That became not only my measuring stick to judge other books by but also a guide as I grew older on how to behave properly towards them. And, yes, I have had real world experiences, some good and some not so much. I've been pixie-led, I've seen fairy hounds both black as night and shining white, I've encountered land spirits of various sorts, and more. For me honoring and interacting with the Fey is done as much out of inevitability as choice, but I can honestly say that it's never been boring.

So who, exactly, do I offer to and how do I see them? The Good Neighbors (the Gentry, the Fair Folk) look much like Tolkien's elves but without the pointed ears and seem to be a kind of cousin of the Norse Alfar. Some of them take an interest in a person or family and will offer help and guidance, even when the person doesn't listen or goes against the helpful advice. With the Fair Folk either they like you or they do not, there is no real influencing it, although they can certainly be angered by anyone. Land spirits often take the form of an animal and sometimes of a person, but seem more primal in their nature than the Fair Folk with their structured culture. In my experience land spirits have a more territorial feeling to them, which immediately sets them apart from other types of fairies, and they seem to prefer more natural offerings. And of course there are also house spirits that can be offered to, and who may appear in diverse forms, usually smaller, and can affect the luck of a home.

Now that I have explained my perspective on Otherworldly beings in general and the Good Neighbors, land spirits and house spirits specifically, on to how I honor them. I have two places I leave offerings, a hawthorn tree in my yard that has been made into a kind of clootie tree and an indoor altar created expressly for the purpose of honoring the aos sidhe, et al. Indoors I will light candles and offer food; they seem to like candy and baked goods, although for the Good Neighbors I sometimes offer jewelry. They also all seem to like milk, cream, and alcohol, with milk and cream being traditional offerings. Outside I will leave baked goods like bread or cakes, and will tie things into the branches of the tree as offerings, such as bells. I make at least one offering each week on a certain day, and additional ones on holy days and special occasions. I also do my best to remember to pay attention and listen, and I have received many useful messages this way; additionally, of course, I interact with them during spiritual journeys when I am traveling out into their space, so to speak.

I follow the belief that we should not say 'thank you' to any being of Faery as it is dismissive and they don't seem to appreciate it. So, when I call them in ritual, which I do, I always end by saying, 'May there be peace and friendship between us.' I always make some sort of offering. And I always do my best to follow the various geasa associated with working with the daoine sidhe and the personal ones I have accumulated. I could not fairly say that I am closer to the daoine sidhe than the ancestors or Gods, but I can say that while the others wax and wane in interest and attention, the Otherworldly spirits are a constant for me. There is probably some irony in that somewhere.

Honoring my Ancestors

I do not know exactly how long I have been honoring my ancestors, although I do know that I began doing so long before I was associating with any groups or formal religions that encourage it; I would guess probably since around the mid 1990s. Of course now I know that many pagan faiths, including heathenry and Druidism, include aspects of honoring the ancestors, both the person's own family line as well as important past figures or close family friends who are not blood relations. There are different reasons for remembering those who have come before – some people do it to keep the memory of those people alive and to nurture a sense of connection to the past; others do it because they believe that a person's spirit lives on after physical death and can be interacted with. I fall into this second group, since I have always believed that the spirit lives on and that there can still be a relationship with these spirits. I don't think my actual practice directly reflects those taught by any one faith group, rather it seems that parts of what I do are a little like what many other groups do.

My initial approach to ancestor worship,[3] which is still a main part of my practice, was to create an ancestor altar. At first this served simply as a way to feel connected to my ancestors, who I had not known in life, but as relatives who I knew and loved began passing away the purpose shifted to a place I could go to talk with them, light candles for them, burn incense, and leave offerings. My first ancestor altars were simple affairs, a small collection of pictures of my relatives, then adding a simple white candle.

As time went on the altar grew and became more complicated, with a decorated resin skull being added in to represent all of my ancestors whose names I did not know, but who were still with me in some sense. I also added a collection of small female statues to represent my Disir, the female ancestors who guard my family line. A special oracle set, and then two, were added for when I felt the need to consult my Dead without wanting to go the full spae route. Many of the pictures acquired little tokens or mementos, usually objects owned by that person in life, and more candles were added. In short the altar developed its own personality.

I like to light the candles on my ancestor altar and talk with my ancestors, especially my father, the way I did when they were still alive. It acts as a touchstone for me, a place I can go to honor my Dead but also a place I can go for comfort. I point each picture out to my children and tell them stories about their ancestors. I bring offerings of coffee (a staple drink in my family!) and of bread. At the holidays that they celebrated I bring candy. I also make spontaneous offerings outside, usually of coffee or hot chocolate, which seem to be the best received; I simply say whatever I feel moved to say and pour a little bit out onto the earth for them.

Speaking of holidays they celebrated – yes my ancestors were Christians; Catholic on my father's side and Congregationalist on my mother's. I have not found this to make any difference whatsoever in their acceptance of my honoring them, although my Catholic grandmother has asked that I have masses said for her, which leads to some interesting experiences on my part. I have certain ancestors who feel closer than others and they seem to be the ones who are more likely to ask for specific things and to come through during divination or spae. Others seem content to be there in the background. Actually it reminds me a lot of the experiences I had with family functions as a child where some people were very chatty and others hung out by the food table snacking, so maybe that's a healthy dynamic to have.

Finally, I have honored my ancestors by doing a variety of genealogical research over the years. I did this to honor their memories, but it also proved to be very enlightening for me, especially for my mother's side, which did not have the tradition of passing down stories of the past generations the way my father's side did. I had known from a young age that my father's mother was half Cherokee and half Scottish, and that his father was the son of a German and an Irish immigrant, for example, and a variety of stories about different family members on that side. But I never knew until I researched that my mother's family had pretty much been in New England since it was a British colony, or that a member of that side of the family had fought in every single American war since the Revolutionary war. It made me feel much more connected to that side of the family. But even if that wasn't possible, even if I had no idea who my parents were or anything else further back, I would still honor them, still acknowledge their place in my life.

The Havamal says:

Cattle die and kinsmen die,
thyself too soon must die,
but one thing never, I ween, will die, –
fair fame of one who has earned

So long as we remember those who have gone before us, whose lives gave us life, they are never really gone. They are our roots, our connection all the way back to the beginnings, and knowing them means knowing ourselves, who we are and where we came from. Even nameless, even unknown, they are still there. I believe they can hear us when we speak to them and that they care about what happens to us, especially those people who loved us in life (blood relations or not). As long as I feel like they are there and care, I will be here, caring, speaking to them, and pouring out offerings for them.

Chapter 3

Holy Days and Celebrations

A Winter Prayer

Scél lemm dúib:
Dordaid dam,
Snigid gaim,
Ro-fáith sam;
Gáeth ard úar,
Ísel grían,
Gair a rith,
Ruirthech rían;
Ro-rúad rath
Ro-cleth cruth,
Ro-gab gnáth
Guigrann guth;
Ro-gab úacht
Etti én
Aigre re
É mo scél.
9th century Irish prayer

A Prayer for the New Year

Bless my two eyes,
May my eyes bless all I see;
I will bless my neighbor,
May my neighbor bless me.

Gods, bless to me this new day,
Never vouchsafed to me before;
As I bless you on this morning,
Embracing the time I am given.

Gods, give me a clean start,
Let me remain under your protection;
Bless my children and my wife (husband),
And bless my life and my possessions.

A Celtic View of Samhain

One of the most widely known pagan holidays is Samhain, a day that is celebrated by Wiccans, Druids and other pagans alike. The modern Samhain has its roots in the ancient Celtic fire festival from which it gets its name, pronounced SOW-en, believed by some to mean 'summer's end'. Samhain is the Irish Gaelic name for the holiday, which is also called Samhuinn in Scottish and Calan Gaiaf in Welsh (Kondratiev, 1998). According to the Gaulish Coligny calendar it is called Trinuoxtion Samonii, which means the 'three nights of summer's end', indicating that the holiday was originally celebrated over a three-day period (Kondratiev, 1998). In modern vernacular, Samhain is called Halloween, abbreviated from All Hallow's Eve, the name given to the holiday by the Christian church. Originally the Catholic holidays that take place on and around Samhain, All Souls and All Saints days, were in February, having been set during the Roman feast of Feralia, but when the Church spread to the Celtic lands the dates were shifted to November.

The Celts celebrated Samhain as the ending of the old year and beginning of the new. Caesar tells us, in his writings about the Gallic War, that the Celts saw the day as well as the New Year beginning at sunset (Freeman, 2002). This would mean that Samhain would have been celebrated starting as the sun went down on one day and continuing on to end at the next sunset. Samhain stood opposite Beltane, and as Beltane marked the beginning of summer, Samhain marked the beginning of winter; moreover as the beginning of the New Year Samhain was probably the most important holiday of the year (McNeill, 1961). The precise dating of Samhain is difficult to determine as it was, like all the Celtic festivals, agrarian based, but it is likely that it would take place around what is now November as this is the time when vegetation dies and the sun is clearly waning (McNeill, 1961). In most modern practices the date is set on October 31st, although some people still celebrate it on November 12th holding to the older date before the transition between the Julian and Gregorian calendars which shifted everything back two weeks (McNeill, 1961).

It is the end of the harvest period, and indeed any produce not gathered in by Samhain is left in the fields (Kandratiev, 1998). This is done because tradition holds that after Samhain night everything left in the fields belongs to the fairies; in some areas the people believed that one fairy in particular, the Púca, went out on Samhain night and claimed all the fruit that was left by urinating on it, or some say spitting on it (Estyn Evans, 1957; McNeill, 1961; Danaher, 1972). At this time as well the herds that were put out to summer pasture at Beltane were brought back in, reuniting the herders with their families and allowing the people to decide how much stock could be kept over the winter and how much should be butchered (Estyn Evans 1957). This was a time for settling debts, and as the last of the harvest fairs ended people would make sure that anything they owed was paid before Samhain (Danaher, 1972). Samhain was a time that was both joyous and eerie, as it was marked by great feasts and community gatherings, but was also a time for telling ghost stories and tales of the fairies stealing people (McNeill, 1961). Today we continue to celebrate with this dual feeling, enjoying the atmosphere of closeness and the visitations by our dead family members, but also relishing the scariness that comes when the veil is so thin. Great bonfires would be lit just as at Beltane and Midsummer. While the Beltane fires were traditionally lit at dawn, the Samhain fires were lit as the sun set as a symbol of the light surviving in the dark (McNeill, 1961). These modern bonfires are carry-overs from the ancient Celtic time when all the fires in each home would be put out and the Druids would light a huge bonfire on a hilltop from which all the other fires would be relit (McNeill, 1961). This practice in Ireland centered on Tara, as it was believed that what was done there would spread outward from the center (Kondratiev, 1998). After all the fires were extinguished the Druids would light a bonfire at Tlachtga, a sacred site near the hill of Tara (Kondratiev, 1998). Even up until the 1970s bonfires were still regularly lit by people on Samhain night in Dublin (Danaher, 1972). In some areas of Ireland when the fires began to die down men and boys would scoop up still-burning embers and throw them at each other, which may possibly be linked to older rituals, although the practice is dangerous (Danaher, 1972). In Scotland the ashes from the bonfires were scattered to fertilize the fields and for protection, since it was believed that they possessed the power to drive away dangerous spirits (McNeill, 1961). In other areas people would blacken their faces with the ashes, believing it was a protection against baneful magic (McNeill, 1961).

Possibly the most prominent theme of Samhain was that of the thinning of the veil between the worlds. On this night the dead could return to visit the living and the fairy hills were opened, releasing all the creatures of fairy into the mortal world (Estyn Evans, 1957; McNeill, 1961). The belief in this was so strong in rural Ireland even up to the last century that it was considered extremely bad luck not to set an extra chair at the table, or put out a bowl of a special porridge, and leave the door to the home open on Samhain (Estyn Evans, 1957). In other accounts the door should be closed but left unlocked and a bowl of fresh water left out by the hearth to welcome any returning family ghosts that choose to visit (Danaher, 1972). In Ireland, however, it is more widely believed that November 2nd is the day when the dead return to visit (Danaher, 1972). This is of particular interest because it may reflect the older practice of celebrating Samhain as a three-day holiday, in which case the return of the dead may have marked the final day of the celebration. In modern practice in Ireland people would light a candle for each deceased member of their family, and in some cases visit the graveyards where they were buried to clean the graves (Danaher, 1972). Although popular imagination paints the idea of the dead returning in a negative light this is not the way the old belief was; in the old practice people didn't fear the dead who came back to visit, but saw them as protective of the living family (Danaher, 1972). It is a very old doctrine of the Celts that the soul is immortal and passes from one life to spirit and then to another life so it would be impossible for the Celts to see Samhain as a holiday devoid of celebration (McNeill, 1961).

Just as all the dead were free to return to earth to visit, so the realm of Faery was opened up, although it has always been a very blurry line between fairies and the dead, as it was often said that some of the dead went to live with the fairies. The denizens of Faery were most likely to be encountered now and it was said that should a person meet a fairy rade and throw the dust from under his feet at them they would be compelled to release any humans they had taken (Danaher, 1972). This night was one of celebration and merry making, but people preferred to travel in groups, fearing that to walk alone on Samhain risked being taken forever into Faery (Danaher, 1972). It was thought that dusk and midnight were particularly dangerous times, and that the fairy troops passed to the west side of homes and along waterways, making it best to avoid these times and places (McNeill, 1961). It was also a long-time custom to shout out 'beware' (seachain!) or 'water towards you' (chughaibh an t-uisce!) if one was tossing water out of the home so that any passing fairies or ghosts would be warned (Danaher, 1972). This is the time that all the fairy raths, or hills, open up and the inhabitants parade from one hill to the next playing music, which some people claim to hear (Danaher, 1972; McNeill, 1961). Anyone who had been kidnapped and taken to Faery could be freed within the first year and a day from when they were taken, but the spells to do so were strongest on Halloween, as we can see in the old tale of Tam Lin (McNeill, 1961). Because the fairies were all abroad it was also the custom in many places to leave them food offerings, but unlike the plates of food left for the dead, the food offerings for fairies took the form of a rich porridge that was made and then placed in a small pit dug in the ground (Sjoestedt, 1949).

Another feature of the celebration is divination for the year to come. One form of such divination was to observe the direction the wind was blowing at midnight, as it was believed that this would indicate the weather of the winter to come (Danaher, 1972). In a similar way the moon, if visible, was used for divination: a clear moon meant good weather, a cloudy moon would be observed and the degree of clouding would represent the amount of rain to come, and clouds passing quickly over the moon's face meant storms (Danaher, 1972). Other folk divinations took on a more homely focus. For example, two hazelnuts or walnuts could be named after a couple and then placed near each other by the edge of the fire and if they stayed together it was a good omen but if the popped or jumped apart it meant the relationship would not last (Danaher, 1972). Apples were also used in a variety of ways, including the modern game of bobbing for apples, which could be used to tell a person's luck in the year to come. Another method to foretell an individual's fortune was to blindfold them and seat them at a table in front of a certain number of plates or bowls, each of which contained something different; the bowl the person touched first indicated something about how their year would go (Danaher, 1972; McNeill, 1961). While these practices are clearly modern they are fully in the spirit of the holiday and using divination to predict the fortunes of a person, and these methods are more easily used today than some of the older ones which focused less on the individual and more on the welfare of the community. In Scotland there was a form of divination that utilized the sacred bonfire; a circle would be made from the ashes of the still-smoldering fire and around this circle of ashes stones would be placed to represent the people present – in the morning should any stone be moved or damaged it indicated doom for that person (McNeill, 1961).

Samhain is also a time in the Celtic world to give thanks for the harvest, and the bounty that had been secured to get the people through the winter. McNeill compares Samhain to saying a prayer of thanks after a meal, just as she sees Beltane as a prayer before a meal (McNeill, 1961). In certain parts of Scotland it was the custom up to the 1600s for the people of a town to gather and each contribute a portion of ale, which one man would then carry out into the ocean as an offering to the sea God, Shony (McNeill, 1961). Another interesting custom is the baking of a special oatmeal cake, which would be prepared with much ceremony and then offered to a stranger (McNeill, 1961). This may be a reflection of older customs of sharing from one's own abundance to ensure more in the future; this is also a reflection of a similar custom from Imbolc where after the feast the remnants were offered to the poor of the community (Carmichael, 1900). Offerings would be made during this time by tossing them into the sacred bonfires, both in thanks for blessings received and symbolizing requests the people would like granted in the New Year (Kondratiev, 1998).

It is likely that the modern practice of Halloween trick or treating comes from older Celtic practices, called guising. In County Cork into the 19th century there was a practice that involved a small procession led by someone dressed as a white mare that would go door to door asking for tolls and singing (Estyn Evans, 1957; Danaher, 1972). In some parts of modern Ireland it is still the practice of trick or treating children to chant, 'Help the Halloween party! Any apples or nuts?' (Danaher, 1972). This request for apples or nuts is almost certainly a reflection of older traditions, as apples are strongly connected to the Otherworld and the hazel was a symbol of occult wisdom

(McNeill, 1961). All through Scotland it was the custom of groups of boys to go out disguised and travel from door to door asking for money or treats, often while singing or chanting (McNeill, 1961). The practice slowly switched to children going out dressed in masks and carrying torches who would repeat chants like, 'Hallowe'en! A nicht o' tine! A can'le in a custock!' (Halloween! A night of fire! A candle in a holder!) or 'Heigh ho for Halloween, when the fairies a' are seen, some black and some green, heigh ho for Halloween!' (McNeill, 1961). Both of these chants reflect the older practices of the pagan holiday in referring to fire and to the fairies being abroad.

Finally, Samhain was also connected to blessing activities and making charms to bless, draw luck, and protect in the year to come, as were all the fire festivals to some degree. In Ireland it was a custom to make a charm very similar to the solar cross of St. Brighid which would be hung on the wall over the inside of the door to ward off all bad luck and harm in the year to come (Danaher, 1972). Infants and children would be sprinkled with blessed water and a piece of iron or a cold ember from the fire was placed under their bed to protect them; in other areas a mix of oatmeal and salt was dabbed on the child's forehead (Danaher, 1972). In Scotland, even up until the 1850s, people would go out on Samhain and make torches from wood or heather and these would be lit from the sacred fire (originally the Druidic fires and later the bonfires lit at home); these torches would be carried around the boundary of the home sun-wise by the family to bless the place (McNeill, 1961).

There are a few specific deities associated with Samhain, which vary by area. In Scotland many believe that it is at Samhain that Brighid turns over control of the year to the Cailleach, who rules then until Imbolc (McNeill, 1961). The Cailleach is in many ways the spirit of winter and of the cold weather, who controls the storms, so her rule during this time of year makes sense. For some people who follow the Tuatha Dé

Danann of Ireland Samhain may be a period to honor the Dagda and the Morrigan, who in mythology were said to have joined together on this date. Indeed, many important events occur on Samhain in Irish mythology.

In modern practice there are many ways to incorporate these ancient traditions, whether you are solitary or celebrate in a group. I recommend celebrating the secular Halloween first, as it is firmly rooted in the ancient practices of guising. Go to a place you consider sacred and create sacred space as you normally would, then call whatever Gods and spirits you feel appropriate for the rite. During the rite itself offerings should be made to the Gods in thanks and to ask for their continued blessing, and porridge may be offered to the fairies. Afterwards you could have a bonfire after putting out any other fires and turning off all the lights, but even if that's not possible, a symbolic bonfire could be made, perhaps in a cauldron, or a large candle lit. Put out all the lights and then relight your sacred fire for the New Year and then small offerings can be made to the fire, both in thanks and with requests for the year to come. One practice that I and several friends use that reflects the old idea of lighting candles for the dead is to carve the names of all those we care about who have passed onto a candle and then light it during a ritual in their honor. Different methods of divination can be done, either based on traditional methods or more modern ones, to see what the year to come might bring. When the rite is done you can either pick up the candle or light a candle or small torch from the ritual fire and walk around your yard or ritual area, clockwise, carrying it to bless the space for the year to come. Then you or your group should have a potluck feast; it might be nice if everyone contributed a dish that held some significance for them or was a family recipe. Portions of this should be set aside for the visiting dead who should be as welcome to attend as the living members. After the feast this plate can be left on the table for the dead, and the candle in their honor can be left burning, if it is safe to do so.

When the celebration is over ashes can be taken from the ritual fire and kept as a protective charm for the year to come.

References:

Carmichael, A., (1900). Carmina Gadelica , volume 1
Danaher, K., (1972). The Year in Ireland.
Estyn Evans, E., (1957). Irish Folk Ways
Freeman, P., (2002). War, Women, and Druids
Kondratiev, A., (1998). The Apple Branch: a Path to Celtic Ritual
McNeill, F., (1961). The Silver Bough, volume 3: Halloween to Yule.
Sjoestedt, M., (1949). Celtic Gods and Heroes

A Family Samhain

Tuesday November 1, 2011

I love this time of year. Halloween has been my favorite holiday for as long as I can remember and when I became pagan I incorporated the practices that I loved about Halloween with the ones I learned went along with Samhain; luckily for me trick-or-treating and dressing up in costume are pretty strongly connected to the old Celtic custom of guising, which have continued until today. In Ireland up until around a hundred years ago there was still a practice of a small parade led by someone dressed as a white mare that would go from house to house singing and asking for 'tolls' (Estyn Evans, 1957; Danaher, 1972). In some parts of modern Ireland children still chant, 'Help the Halloween party! Any apples or nuts?' when trick or treating (Danaher, 1972). All through Scotland it was the custom of groups of boys in costume to go door to door asking for money or treats, often while singing or chanting which slowly became the custom of younger children that we consider trick-or-treating in modern times (McNeill, 1961).

I took my children out trick-or-treating, with the girls dressed up as Cleopatra and a pirate queen respectively. It was extremely fun being out at night with the children, under the crescent moon, with the snap of snow in the air. We had actually had an unusual early snow storm last Saturday that knocked out power and generally mucked things up for awhile, but by yesterday everything was enchanted.

Now the modern dating of Samhain is given as October 31st and this is when I choose to celebrate it for convenience, but in reality the date was originally not a set calendar or astrological date, as far as we know, but rather was an agrarian date in Ireland and Scotland; although the Coligny calendar of Gaul does list three specific days as 'Trinuoxtion Samonii' or the three nights of summers end (Kondratiev, 1999). In practice Samhain celebrations occurred in November because this was the end of the harvest and the time when the herds were brought back in from the fields, but it wasn't until the Catholic Church moved its celebration of All Saints and All Souls day to the first days of November that Samhain seem to have gotten a set calendar date in a modern context (Estyn Evans, 1957; McNeill, 1961). Of course then the switch was made from the Julian to Gregorian calendar and so you still see people celebrating Samhain on November 12th, refusing to acknowledge the change (McNeill, 1961). I debated for awhile trying to hold to a more traditional agrarian marking of the date, perhaps at the first hard frost each year, but with the kids it was just too difficult to get them engaged and excited about it when it seemed random to them. I do, however, follow what Caesar said about the Celts starting the new day at sunset and the new year at Samhain and begin my celebrations at sunset of the 31st and I also generally make it a three-day celebration, something that is supported by the Coligny calendar and at least tenuously by the Irish belief that it was actually on November 2nd that the spirits of the dead returned to visit the living (Freeman, 2002; Danaher, 1972).

After trick-or-treating we came home and had a small

ceremony together. We lit a candle for those we love who have passed on and talked about them, things we remembered and missed.

It was an old practice in Ireland to light a candle for each deceased member of the family and to leave the doors unlocked – in some cases even open – and to leave out either fresh water or porridge as an offering to those ancestors who chose to visit (Estyn Evans, 1957; Danaher, 1972). Lighting the candle carved with their names is our way of carrying on this tradition. Then, in honor of the idea of leaving out food for the dead, we took a cake that we had baked earlier in the day and put pieces outside for the Gods, daoine sidhe, and ancestors, all in different places, as well as leaving out something for any wandering spirits. And we went back inside and each had a little piece of cake ourselves. Then the children went to bed and I did some divination on my own.

Tonight is the second night of my Samhain celebration. I will honor the Morrigan and the Dagda who united on Samhain, and who are both deities I am personally close to. I will kindle a sacred fire, symbolically relighting the fire of my hearth and of the world[4] and I will do some more divination and make charms to bless my home in the coming year; Samhain was associated with a solar cross charm similar to the Brighid's cross of Imbolc and with using fire to sain, or bless, the property (Danaher, 1972; McNeill 1962). Tomorrow will be focused especially on honoring the dead and on blessing the people of the house for the year to come using the ashes of tonight's fire. And then Samhain will be over for another year.

References:

Danaher, K., (1972). The Year in Ireland

Estyn Evans, E., (1957). Irish folk Ways

Freeman, P., (2002). War, Women, and Druids

Kondratiev, A., (1998). The Apple Branch: a path to Celtic Ritual

McNeill, F., (1961). The Silver Bough, volume 3: Halloween to Yule

My Gaelic Heathen Yule

Thursday, December 15, 2011

So Yule is fast approaching, and this Yule will represent my first attempt at incorporating some Celtic elements and traditions into what has so far been a Germanic and Norse festival period for me. Prior to becoming heathen in 2006 I didn't celebrate the winter solstice in any special way, beyond the secular; after becoming heathen I began celebrating the 'traditional' 12 days of Yule, beginning on Mother Night and ending usually either on New Year's Eve or New Year's Day. I followed the Celtic reconstructionist approach of celebrating the four Irish fire festivals as holidays and not acknowledging any Celtic aspects of the solstices or equinoxes. However, this year I am looking at what the more modern Celtic traditions of this time of year are and how they may relate to older heathen ones in order to create a more synchretic personal approach (celebrating with my kindred is still Norse oriented).

In Germanic and Norse traditions Yule is a 13-night, 12-day festival that is considered one of the most sacred times of the year. Yule begins on Mother Night, the night before the solstice, which is often celebrated in honor of Frigga and the disir; in my family we celebrate Mother Night two days before the calendar date of the solstice because the eve of Yule has developed its own family traditions. Many modern heathens that I know choose to stay up on the night before the solstice in order to greet the dawn on the solstice morning. The day of the solstice itself is considered both the most powerful of Yule and also the most dangerous as both trolls and ghosts are roaming free on the night of Yule. On this day the Yule log is burnt and the most sacred oaths are sworn. Celebrations continue until New Year's Day, a day that itself is important since it sets the tone for the year to come; actions taken on the last day of Yule/New Year's Eve (or Day) influence the year to come.

Swearing oaths and making sacred toasts were sacred activities, as well as leaving out food offerings for the Gods and spirits. Odin was especially associated with Yule time, as are the Goddesses Perchte, Berchte or Holda. Yule bucks were made (the mask of a goat head, or a straw goat) and used for guising, but the Yule buck was also believed to have its own separate spirit that had to be propitiated – often with ale or porridge – in order not to harm anyone in the family. Porridge is also left out as an offering to the house wight or spirit that lives in the home. A Yule tree was used for decoration and a Yule log was burnt, or in some modern cases a log is set with candles which are burnt.

Now working with that as a base we can look at what we have for Yule traditions in Scotland. In Scotland McNeill states that while Odin may be known as the Yule Father it is Thor to whom this holiday actually belongs, as does all of the month of December. A Yule log of oak was traditionally burnt and Thor was asked to bring a prosperous new year. She relates a story of Norsemen in Scotland celebrating Yule with a great feast and then a bonfire, around which they danced and then chanted, 'Thor with us, Thor and Odin! Haile Yule, haile!' (McNeill, 1961, p. 52). In Scotland the 'Christmas' season ran from Christmas Eve until Twelfth Night, reflecting the older heathen practice of a 12-day celebration of Yule. Prior to the start of Yule the home was cleaned from top to bottom and stocked with food. During the period of Yule all household work like spinning and weaving was strictly prohibited as it was believed that to do such work, even drawing water, during the 12 days of Yule would risk the girls of the house being taken by a Kelpie. The hearth was cleaned and decorated to please the Gods and garlanded with rowan to keep out mischievous spirits. On the eve of Yule the family would go out and collect the Yule log which would be brought in with great ceremony, an offering of ale was poured over it, and it was placed in the fire to burn through the night. In some parts of the Highlands the Yule log is associated with the Cailleach, the spirit of winter, and in those places the Yule log chosen would be the stump of an old tree. Special breads and cakes were baked on Yule eve, and ale and sowans were made with omens taken from how they cooked. First thing on Yule morning weather omens were taken to predict the year to come; green Yule meant snow in spring, warm Yule a cold spring, and a light Yule a good harvest. The rest of the day was spent in social gatherings and feasting. Another Yule tradition is guisers and mummers who travel from house to house in costume singing and offering entertainment and blessings in exchange for welcome into the home and some food.

New Year's Eve, called Hogmany, has many traditions of its own, including special cleaning of the home, settling any debts, returning borrowed items, and generally setting everything in the household right in preparation for the New Year. At the exact stroke of midnight on New Year's Eve the head of the household opens the front door and lets the old year out while welcoming the New Year in with the words, 'Welcome in New Year! When ye come, bring good cheer!' (McNeill, 1961, p. 104). Another important tradition of New Year's Day is first footing, or the belief that the first non-family member who enters the home after midnight on New Year's Day will indicate the family's luck in the coming year, with a cheerful dark haired man being the best first-footer, and a pretty woman being second best. Anyone born with a deformity, of bad character, who is stingy, whose eyebrows meet in the middle, or who may have the Evil Eye are bad luck. To avert the ill luck of a bad first footing throw salt in the fire, burn a wisp of straw, or put a burning coal in water.

In Scotland, New Year is also a time of blessing the home and of omens. Holly, hazel, and rowan were hung up around the home and the entire home was fumigated with burning juniper.

Burning the juniper was considered very important to cleanse the home and was done immediately upon waking before anyone ate breakfast. On New Year's Eve a silver coin was left out on the doorstep and if it was still there in the morning it was seen as a sign of prosperity for the year to come, but if it was gone it was an ill omen. Wearing new clothes on New Year's Day was good luck so was carrying a silver coin in your pocket. To see a red dawn on New Year's Day meant bad luck and strife to come, and the direction of the wind was an omen of the year to come as well: 'Wind from the west, fish and bread, wind from the north, cold and flaying, wind from the east, snow on the hills, wind from the south, fruit on trees.' (McNeill, 1961, p. 115).

In Ireland, Yule was also started with a complete cleaning of the home, which was followed by decorating with holly, ivy, bay and other evergreens, and as in Scotland, food was stocked up. Preparations were made that included placing lit candles in the windows of the home; these are now associated with Christmas but may well be older as some believe the candles' light serves to guide and welcome the visiting dead who wander at this time of year. Some choose to light a special candle for any family members who have passed in the last year. As in Scotland the weather is seen as being an omen of the year to come with cold weather foretelling a warm spring; additionally a new moon was seen as especially lucky. Mumming and guising was also seen and New Year's Eve and Day were strongly associated with divination and omens.

While first footing isn't seen in Ireland the way it is in Scotland, there is a belief that if the first person or animal to enter the home after midnight on New Year's Eve is male and black or dark haired the house will have good luck. A special bread was traditionally baked and then hit three times against the door while the head of the house or house wife chanted either, 'We warn famine to retire, to the country of the Turks, from this night to this night twelvemonth, and even this very night,' or,

'Happiness in and misfortune out from this night, until a year from tonight.' (Danaher, 1972, p. 261). After this the loaf was tossed out the door.

So this actually gives us a lot to work with for celebrating both Germanic/Norse Yule traditions and Celtic ones over the course of a 12-day celebration. I like the idea of including Thor more in the Yule celebrations, especially as they relate to the Yule log, and of lighting candles for my ancestors, which I may do each night of Yule. Including the Cailleach makes sense as well. I also can easily see how to incorporate the specific New Year's Eve and Day traditions, such as welcoming the New Year in and also the Irish custom of banging the bread on the door. And the multitude of divinations and omens can easily be used on the day of Yule and on New Year's Day, as can the cleaning of the home before the start of Yule and the cleansing and blessing rituals of New Year's Day.

I'm excited to see how Yule this year is going to go as I work on finding the synergy of this path, which clearly has so much potential.

References:

The Troth, (2007). Our Troth volume 2
Danaher, K., (1972). The Year in Ireland
McNeill, F., (1961). The Silver Bough volume 3

Imbolc: Traditional Celebrations for a Modern Time

This holiday is called many names including Imbolc, Oímealg, Lá Fhéile Bríde, Laa'l Breeshey, and Gwyl Mair Dechrau'r Gwanwyn and was originally celebrated when the ewes first began to lactate. Some older sources mention Imbolc being celebrated on February 13th, although now the date is fixed on February 2nd. This holiday is a celebration of the loosening of winter's hold on the land and the first signs of spring's imminent arrival. Three main types of ceremonies could be undertaken – purification with water, blessing with fire, and consecration of talismans or charms. In addition the main ritual theme centered on inviting the Goddess Brighid into the home, either in effigy or in the form of a person acting the part.

The fire represents the growing light of the sun. Candles would be lit to celebrate the increased daylight, and often candles were blessed for use in the year to come; this connection to candles offers another alternate name for the holiday, Candlemas. In my personal practice I light special 'sun' candles, and bless my candle holders for the year to come.

Ritual washing was done to cleanse and prepare the people for the agricultural work of the coming seasons. Water was blessed and then used to ceremonially wash the head, hands, and feet. Each year when I do this I dip my fingers in the blessed water and run them over the body parts in question, asking that I be cleansed of winter's cold and filled with summer's warmth to work towards a new season. Then I pour the remaining water out onto the earth thanking Brighid for her blessing.

The main charms and talismans of Imbolc are related to Brighid. First there is the Brighid's cross, a woven sun wheel shape which represented the cycle of the year and the four main holy days, according to the book Apple Branch. On Imbolc you can weave new Brighid's crosses, or bless ones you already have, although it may be better to burn the old and weave new each year when possible. A Brighid's cross is protective and healing to have in the home.

A second talisman is the brídeóg, or 'little Brighid' a small cloth or straw doll wearing white clothes which is an effigy of the Goddess. In some cases the brídeóg would be made from straw saved from the previous Lughnasadh. This doll played a role in ritual after being taken outside, usually carried by the eldest daughter, then invited to enter the home where it was led with all ceremony to a specially prepared little bed. The doll was left in the bed overnight and its presence was believed to bless all those in the household.

Another talisman connected to Imbolc in Ireland is Brigid's mantle, or 'an brat Bríd', a length of cloth left out on the windowsill over the course of the holy day and night. It is believed that this cloth absorbs the energy of the Goddess during the ritual, and can be used for healing and protection throughout the year. This talisman would be kept and recharged every year, attaining full power after seven years.

The ritual for Brighid on Imbolc centers on inviting the Goddess in and offering her hospitality. In some cases a woman was chosen to play the part of the Goddess, in other cases the brídeóg was used. The door would be opened to her and she would loudly be invited in, shown to her 'bed' and offered specially baked bread. Candles would be lit at the windows and next to her 'bed', songs would be sung and prayers said calling on Brighid to bless all present in the coming seasons, and grant health and protection to the household. In Scotland a small broom or white wand would be placed next to the bed, and the ashes from the fire would be smoothed down in the hopes that the morning would reveal the marks of the wand, or better yet, the footprints of the Goddess herself, either of which would be a sign of blessing. Placing the doll in her bed at night would be followed by a large family meal. In Scotland a hundred years ago when entire communities still celebrated Imbolc in the old way, a sheaf of corn would be dressed as Brighid and taken from house to house by the young girls. The girls would carry the doll from home to home where the 'Goddess' would be greeted and offered food and gifts. After visiting each home the girls would return to the house they started from where a party would be held with music, dancing, and feasting until dawn; all the leftover food would be handed out to the poor the next day.

Other rituals involve blessing the forge fires for blacksmiths and Otherworld divinations. In some Scottish mythologies it is believed that Brighid is held by the Cailleach Bhur during the winter months but escapes, or is rescued by her brother Angus mac Og, on Imbolc. In others it is said the Cailleach drinks from a hidden spring and transforms into Brighid on this day.

For modern people seeking to celebrate Imbolc in a traditional way there are many options. Rituals can be adapted to feature the brídeóg. If you celebrate in a group you could have one person wait outside with the doll while the other members prepare her bed, and then the group leader could go to the doorway and invite the Goddess in. This could even be modified for use in an urban setting with the brídeóg 'waiting' out in a hallway or separate room to be invited in. Once invited in the Goddess can be offered food and gifts as was done in Scotland and stories about Brighid from mythology could be told. Water can be used for purification, blessing with fire or of candles can be done, as well as making and consecrating the charms associated with Brighid. After the ritual the doll could be left in the bed while the group celebrates with a party; to keep the spirit of the way this was done for a modern time all members should bring food to donate to a local food pantry. A solitary celebration could still include inviting the Goddess in, placing the brídeóg in her bed, making offerings to her, and a private celebration and food donations.

Imbolc is a powerful holy day with many beautiful traditions. By understanding how this day was celebrated in the past we can find ways to incorporate those methods into modern practice and preserve the traditions that have surrounded Brighid's day for so many generations.

References:

Carmichael, A., (1900). Carmina Gadelica

Evert Hopman, E., (1995). A Druid's Herbal of the Sacred Earth Year

Kondrariev. K., (1998). The Apple Branch: A Path to Celtic Ritual

McNeill, F., (1959). The Silver Bough, volume 2

A Beltane Prayer

Danu, mother of the people of skill,
Bless our home and all within;
Do not let hate and curses come near us,
Drive from us the ways of the wicked.

Keep your eyes every Monday and Tuesday
On our house and possessions and lives;
Accompany us from hill to sea,
Gather us in under your golden cloak.

Every Wednesday and Thursday be with us,
Your gracious hands always about us;
Watch over us as we work,
Watch over us as we rest!

Every Friday be at our head,
Lead us away from any danger,
And protect our helpless little children from harm,
Encompass us with your encompassing.

Every Saturday be likewise with us,
Bring to us luck and prosperity,
As we travel to the sea side,
And from the Rock of Aegir on high,
With tresses green about its summit.
The strength of Morrighan be our shield in distress,
The strength of Brighid, her peace and her passion,
The strength of Airmed, gentle healer,
And of the Good God, Daghda, wisest of all.
And of every other God in kinship with them
And who is one of the people of Danu.

Bless ourselves and our children,
Bless every one who shall come from our loins,
Bless him whose name we bear,
Bless, O Gods her from whose womb we came.
Every holiness, blessing and power,
Be yielded to us every time and every hour,
In name of the Gods of life,
By land, sea, and sky.

Be the blessing of Morrighan to shield us downward,
Be the blessing of Morrighan to shield us upward,
Be the blessing of Morrighan to shield us roundward,
Accepting our Beltane blessing from us,
Accepting our Beltane blessing from us.
Modified from the Carmina Gadelica

Beltane: Blessing the Summer In

To the pagan Celts, Bealtine (pronounced roughly Ball-tinn-eh), often called Beltane by modern pagans, was one of the most sacred times. The people of Ireland and Scotland celebrated Beltane as one of the most important holidays of the year even up until recently. Also called Bealltainn in Scotland and Bealtaine as well as Bealtine in Ireland, this holiday is generally celebrated on May 1st and might also be called May Day, although some people believe in celebrating it based on environmental signs, such as the blooming of the hawthorn. It is uncertain what the name Beltane means; some people theorize that it translates to 'fires of Bel' while others favor the meaning 'blessing fires'.

Beltane stood opposite Samhain on the calendar and in many ways represented opposite themes; where Samhain was a time of harvest and of the dead, Beltane was a time of blessing and planting (McNeill, 1959). It was on Beltane that the herds were sent out to their summer pastures, and in the old stories it was on Beltane that many important events occurred such as the

Tuatha Dé Danann first arriving in Ireland. It is said that in ancient Ireland all fires were put out on the eve of Beltane and then the Druids would light a sacred fire at Tara which would be passed from hilltop to hilltop and home to home until all the fires were re-lit (Wilde, 1991).

Beltane is the beginning of summer and was the time that contracts were renewed, herds moved, and crops planted. For modern pagans, especially Celtic pagans, a great deal of depth can be added to the celebration of this holiday by understanding the folk traditions surrounding it.

The fairies were thought to be especially active and powerful on Beltane, and in some sources for the first three days of May. It was said in Ireland that it was on Beltane eve that the fairies moved from one hill to another and were most likely to steal children or cause mischief (Danaher, 1972). Caution was needed to guard against fairies stealing the household's luck, dairy products, or herbs, and the best protection against this was strewing primroses across the threshold (Wilde, 1991). This belief also meant that strangers were looked on with great suspicion, lest they actually be fairies in disguise, and there were strong prohibitions against giving away or lending milk or fire on Beltane. Offerings of food might be made to appease the fairies, or else a bit of iron or rowan would be carried as protection (Danaher, 1972).

In Scotland on Beltane all of the hearth fires were extinguished and the people, along with their livestock, would gather before dawn on hilltops where bonfires had been built. The bonfires were built in two large piles so that a narrow path ran between them, and at dawn the fires would be lit (McNeill, 1959). These Beltane bonfires were intended to bless those who passed between them, both people and animals, and were made from sacred woods, in some places oak and in others traditionally nine different woods (McNeill, 1959). As soon as the fire was lit, the people would proceed sunwise around the hilltop three times before driving the animals three times between the bonfires to bless them; later the men would light torches made of heather or sedge and carry them around the animals to protect them from evil and ensure fertility of the herds (McNeill, 1959). After the bonfires subsided the people would rub the ashes on their faces to bless themselves, before proceeding with living embers back to their homes to rekindle their hearth fires; such fire was said to be blessed for a full year and was not allowed to go out until the following Beltane (McNeill, 1959). In the Shetland Islands the Beltane fires were kept burning for three days and people would leap through them for blessing and good health (McNeill, 1959).

In Ireland up to fairly recent times, bonfires were a large public affair that occurred on the night of Beltane, although the practices are dying out today. These fires were traditionally true bonfires, or 'bone-fires', made with a mix of wood and the bones of cows and horses as well as the horns of cows (Evans, 1957). The fires would be built in open public spaces and the people would gather, whether or not they had celebrated earlier, and drink and sing around the fire (Danaher, 1972). It seems that originally the bonfire traditions were common in every town and village but over time slowly died out in many areas. According to the oldest stories and myths, during the pagan period all the home fires would be put out and relit from a great central fire kindled by the Druids on Beltane morning. In modern practice the bonfires would be jumped over to increase a person's fertility and show their bravery (Evans, 1957). In earlier times, just as in Scotland, the fire would have been built in two halves and the livestock driven through the middle, as well as the ash from the Beltane fire used to bless the fields (Danaher, 1972).

In Scotland up until a hundred years ago, folk celebrations included the making of a small fire and cooking of caudle, a mix of eggs, butter, milk, and oatmeal, with every participant contributing something to the celebration and the very first of the prepared food being poured out onto the earth as an offering

(McNeill, 1959). Special cakes were prepared, and then each person would turn their back to the fire and break off pieces of the cake, while naming first a protective deity or spirit that watched over the herds and then a harmful animal that might threaten the herds, the piece would then be tossed over their shoulder into the fire (McNeill, 1959).

In a different part of Scotland, boys would gather on Beltane and make a small fire and then draw lots after which one of them would have to jump three times over the fire as a symbolic sacrifice to the pagan God Bel (McNeill, 1959). Special oat or barley cakes, called Beltane bannocks, were baked and eaten for luck and health, with a small portion given first as an offering that the person may receive abundance (McNeill, 1959).

Both fire and water were used for blessing and as the bonfires were created to bless the herds and people, so too was water collected for blessing. Holy wells might be visited, with due ceremony, and the person might wash in the well or take a small amount of water home with them. In Ireland, the first water drawn from a well, called 'the top of the well' or 'the luck of the well', was believed to be especially powerful for either good or bad intent (Danaher, 1972). Another practice in both Ireland and Scotland was the collection of the dew on Beltane morning, as it was believed that this water had special healing and blessing properties.

In Scotland, special hollows in rocks were found, or alternately a rope made of cow hair was used to gather the dew (McNeill, 1959). A girl might go out and gather dew-covered ivy on Beltane for luck, but it could not be touched with a steel knife or the luck would leave it (McNeill, 1959). In Ireland the dew was collected by hand or by soaking a linen cloth on dew-soaked grass and then ringing out the cloth (Danaher, 1972).

The rowan was central in many Scottish celebrations as it was believed that it was the best protector against the fairies, with rowan branches collected on the eve of Beltane and hung up around the home, or tied with red thread and hung over the door (McNeill, 1959). In one part of Scotland a hoop was made of rowan and then all the sheep were driven through it, while in another a rowan twig and red thread were tied to the cows' tails (McNeill, 1959). In Ireland, rowan is believed to be the best of all protections against bad luck and enchantment, so on May Day morning a branch of rowan might be woven into the ceiling to protect the house and all within it for the next year (Danaher, 1972). One ceremony noted from Laois Ireland called for the head of the family to light a candle and bless the door, hearth, and the four corners of the home, as well as each family member from oldest to youngest, and then the area around the home where a rowan branch should be placed (Danaher, 1972).

In Ireland, it has been the custom for the children to gather flowers on May eve, possibly a holdover of the people once going out before dawn on May morning; these flowers were then hung up or strewn around the home for luck (Danaher, 1972). On May Day itself, flowers were tied to the bridles of horses and the horns of cows for the same purpose (Danaher, 1972). Flowers were also gathered and used to decorate wells, in order to bless and protect them (Evans, 1957). In Munster, a selection of wood boughs were gathered, generally of holly, hazel, elder, rowan, and ash, while in Munster it was sycamore (Danaher, 1972). In contrast, the boughs from fairy trees like blackthorn were seen as extremely unlucky in one area but might be lucky in another. However, the general belief was not to disturb the fairy trees.

Any herbs gathered on Beltane were believed to be especially potent. Yarrow, a herb already believed to be good for nearly anything, was seen as being ideal if gathered on Beltane (Wilde, 1991). No herb, however, could be gathered with an iron knife because the iron would ruin any magical properties held by the plant. Plants gathered on May Day were ideally gathered at dawn with the dew still on them, as the dew itself also imparted a blessing (Wilde, 1991). All charms and magics were most powerful on Beltane so it was also believed to be a time when witches were most active (Danaher, 1972; Wilde 1991).

Another Irish custom was the preparation of a female effigy, called the 'May Baby' that was bedecked with flowers and paraded around the town or village; some theorize that this is an older pagan element related to honoring a Goddess (Danaher, 1972). As the May Baby was carried around music was played and a married couple, chosen beforehand, danced in a comically sexual manner around the effigy to entertain it; this procession was believed to grant fertility to the land and the people who observed it, and belief in its efficacy was so strong that married women without children were known to travel great distances to receive this blessing (Danaher, 1972). A related practice was the May Boys, a troupe of boys or young men that traveled around singing songs like:

Summer! Summer! The milk of the heifers,
And ourselves brought the summer with us,
The yellow summer, the white daisy,
And ourselves brought the summer with us!

A widespread Irish custom was the placement of a 'May bush', a branch or bough of a tree (sometimes a hawthorn or holly) that was placed by the front door for luck and decorated with yellow flowers, brightly colored ribbons, and egg shells (Danaher, 1972). On the night of May Day candles might be lit on or around the bush and people would gather and dance around it; in Ireland in previous centuries large parties were held which included feasting and music (Danaher, 1972). The bush itself might be left standing all month, or until the decorations began falling apart, or in some areas was burned in the night-time bonfire (Danaher, 1972).

One of the Scottish divination practices of Beltane is very similar to one seen at Samhain, where stones are chosen and marked to represent the people present and then placed in a ring around the sacred fire as it is going out – the condition of each stone the next day tells the person's fate (McNeill, 1959). Another practice was to go out before dawn, in silence, and gather yarrow wherever it could be found; it was gathered with the eyes shut and after being picked the person would open their eyes and what they saw would be portentous (McNeill, 1959).

In Ireland divination on Beltane focused largely on the weather for the coming growing season. The direction that the wind was blowing on Beltane day would indicate whether the summer would be a good one or a bad one, and in some areas snow still visible on Beltane was seen as a very bad omen (Danaher, 1972). Another Irish practice was to sweep the threshold clean and then lightly scatter ashes over it; in the morning a footprint coming into the home meant a marriage, while one leaving meant a death in the family in the coming year (Wilde, 1991).

There is little historical evidence of any specific deity associated with Beltane, although in Scotland Bel has come to be connected to the holiday and some of its practices. It is a holiday with strong themes of blessing and fertility, so a modern practitioner could choose to honor any deity or deities that made sense with that energy. This will likely come down to personal preference and probably vary widely by group or person.

For modern practitioners all of this provides a wealth of possible practices to incorporate. Offerings can be made to the fairies to avoid their mischief and encourage friendly relations with the Good Neighbors; this could be done on Beltane eve or Beltane itself. If you choose not to make offerings then perhaps carrying a bit of iron or rowan would be wise to keep the fairies from stealing your luck. In the morning dew could be gathered as well as any useful herbs that can be found.

A May Bush could be set up and decorated, or a live tree or bush could be planted and decorated for the same purpose. The decorations themselves could be the traditional flowers, colorful ribbons, and eggshells, or could be anything else the person imagines that fit the general theme of the holiday. If possible on Beltane night a bonfire is made and danced around or jumped; if it's possible to make two bonfires, they could be passed between for blessing.

Last year at a public ritual I helped co-ordinate we were indoors so we used two candles to mimic two bonfires and processed between those while a blessing prayer was recited. In general the atmosphere of Beltane is one of celebration and merriment, so a party with music, dancing, and as much fun as possible would be entirely in line with this holiday's history.

References:

Danaher, (1972). The Year in Ireland
Evans, E., (1957). Irish Folk Ways
McNeill, F., (1959). The Silver Bough, volume 2
Wilde, (1991). Irish Cures, Mystic Charms and Superstitions

Summer Introspection

Thursday, June 21, 2012

I am not a summer person. While everyone else might be out at the beach, at barbecues, hiking, or otherwise enjoying the outdoors I'm avoiding the bright sunlight and heat by holing up inside. I've always been like this; I was the kid in high school who spent my summers staying up until 4 a.m. reading and watching reruns of classic TV shows and bad B-movies. Each year I dread the returning heat, the oppressive humidity, the bugs and glaring sunshine. Winter is my season, my time to get out and explore the world and enjoy nature – summer is something to be endured. However, I have always tried to force myself to go along with the general expectations, the wider view of summer and the season's energies. People talk about summer as a time for planting and growing, and despite my own desire to do the opposite for many years I pushed against my inclinations. I planted when I wanted to harvest. I nurtured and grew when I wanted to withdraw and contemplate.

I've been thinking about this a lot the past two days as I celebrated Midsummer and as my area experiences a heat wave that has rendered the outdoor atmosphere into something reminiscent of an oven. Online people are talking about the time of year as a time of activity and exploration, in contrast to winter as a time of introspection and withdrawal. What I've come to realize is that for myself these cycles are reversed; to me summer is a time of introspection, when the pace of everything slows down and I look within to sort through what to keep and what to let go of. Fall is a time for returning to the world, for setting new goals as I wait for the leaves to turn and seek the scent of wood smoke in the air. Winter is when I get out the most, walking, hiking, exploring; a time to begin new projects and add effort to old ones. And spring is when things begin to slow down, although there is a rush to finish up what's been begun.

I'm moving into that time of introspection now, assessing and reviewing my life, trying to decide what is worth keeping and what needs to be let go of. One thing I've already come to realize is that I need to start appreciating and honoring my own cycles and patterns instead of trying to fit myself into other people's preconceived cycles. What works for other people may not work for me, but there is no reason I can't find value in my own natural rhythms and learn to appreciate what does work for me. I can appreciate the larger concepts of the accepted cycles of the year while simultaneously honoring my own energetic cycles.

I am not a summer person, and that's okay. I will spend the next few months in introspection and emerge in the fall ready to move forward with renewed energy and purpose.

Midsummer

Saturday, June 23, 2012

Midsummer is a challenge in Irish paganism because there is very limited evidence of its historic practice. However, I like the idea of acknowledging the solstices and of having the balance between summer and winter celebrations. Some summer solstices I have gone in a Norse direction and honored Sunna, but last year and this year I chose to honor Áine, who has long been honored with a torchlit procession on the night of the solstice.

We have had a family tradition of baking cakes on the solstices for many years. At the summer solstice we bake the cake for the daoine sidhe and Áine, who may be a fairy queen or may be a Goddess; and at the winter solstice we bake a cake for the Sun's birthday. In previous years with a more recon-based approach we would bake the summer cake and leave pieces as offerings, but otherwise we didn't do too much to mark the day. Last year I did a public ritual in a more neopagan style that honored the fairies, spirits of the land, and Gods.

This year I combined holiday fun with necessity I gave the gift of new summer shoes to the girls (and my husband), something I might keep as a tradition in the future. We baked a vanilla cake with butter cream frosting and the girls decorated it with candy sprinkles from the store. The cake came out very nicely, and after dinner when everything was ready we sang a Jana Runnall's song called 'Graine' that I learned from an awesome pagan folk singer named Kellianna; then I cut a piece of cake for the fairies and another for Áine. The cake was left outside by our little hawthorn tree and then we went back in and enjoyed some cake ourselves. I read the girls a book about the summer solstice by Ellen Jackson that includes folklore and traditions from around the world.

Later that night I had my own ritual, more official and structured. I would like to be able to include the children in more formal practices, but they still lack patience for anything that isn't active. But this year went well anyway, it was fun, the girls enjoyed it, and the fairies got their cake.

Cake recipe:

1 cup white sugar
½ cup butter
2 eggs
2 teaspoons vanilla extract
1 ½ cups all-purpose flour
1 ¾ teaspoons baking powder
½ cup milk
Preheat oven to 350 degrees F.

Grease and flour a 9x9 inch pan.

In a medium bowl, mix together the sugar and butter. Beat in the eggs then stir in the vanilla. Combine flour and baking powder, add to the mixture and mix well. Finally stir in the milk until batter is smooth. Pour or spoon batter into the prepared pan.

Bake for 30 to 40 minutes in the preheated oven.

Frosting recipe:

½ cup butter, softened
4 ½ cups confectioners' sugar
1 ½ teaspoons vanilla extract
5 tablespoons whole milk

In a large bowl, blend butter until light and fluffy. Beat in the confectioners' sugar, vanilla and enough milk to achieve desired consistency.

A Prayer for Lughnasa

This is based on the Carmina Gadelica, but modernized and made pagan...

Reaping Blessing 89

Gods may you bless my reaping,
Each ridge, and plain, and field,
Each sickle curved, shapely, hard,
Each ear and handful in the sheaf,
Each ear and handful in the sheaf.
Bless each maiden and youth,
Each woman and tender child,
Safeguard them beneath your shield of strength,
And guard them beneath the shadow of your power,
Guard them beneath the shadow of your power.
Encompass each goat, sheep and lamb,
Each cow and horse, and store,
Surround the rocks and herds,
And tend them in a kindly fold,
Tend them in a kindly fold.
May Lugh, the many skilled, bless us,
May Danu's blessing flow to us,
May Brighid of curling locks bless us,
And our ancestors of the graves and tombs,
and our ancestors of the graves and tombs.

Lughnasa, Festival of the Harvest

Lughnasa is also called Lughnasadh, Lunasa, Bron Trogain, Lunsadal, Laa Luanys, Calan Awst, and Gouel an Eost, and Alexei Kondratiev conjectures that the Celts of Gaul may have called this celebration Aedrinia (Kondratiev, 1998). The Irish name of the festival, Lughnasadh or Lughnasa, can be broken down into Lugh Nasadh and translated into either Middle or Old Irish as the assembly of Lugh or the funeral assembly of Lugh. The connection to a funeral assembly undoubtedly references the belief that the celebration was originally created by the God Lugh as a memorial for his foster mother, Tailtiu, after her death, and the assembly of Lugh is thought to refer to the many athletic games and competitions associated with the harvest fairs that occurred at this time. Several of the other names for the holiday are references to the beginning of autumn or of the harvest.

Of the four fire festivals of the Irish Celts Lughnasa has some of the least mythical associations, appearing only in the Lebor Gabála Érenn as the date that the Fir Bolg invaded Ireland (MacNeill, 1962). In modern practice Lughnasa is celebrated on August 1st. However, there is evidence that the date of Lughnasa would actually have represented the starting date of a series of festivals and fairs, rather than a single, one-day celebration with harvest fairs associated with Lughnasadh, called Oenacha, which themselves may last for several days, appearing as late as August 12th (MacNeill, 1962). In modern Irish the word Lunasa means both the first of August and is the name for the entire month of August. It is also the practice on the Isle of Man to celebrate Lughnasa, or Laa Luanys as it is called there, on August 12th every year, likely due to the discrepancy created when the calendar shifted from the Julian to the Gregorian, and there are also some hints that the dates may be hard to pin down because they were originally based on a lunar reckoning that is now lost (MacNeill, 1962). It is generally agreed though that no harvesting should be done before the correct date, represented by Lughnasa, and that to harvest before Lughnasa is both bad luck and the sign of a bad farmer or poor housewife (Danaher, 1972). This folk belief persisted even into the 20th century and indicates the strong connection between Lughnasa and the harvest.

There are several themes surrounding this celebration that include the mundane, the spiritual, and the blending of both. Lughnasa celebrates, at its core, the beginning of the harvest and the new abundance of food being gathered; because of this it is strongly associated with the cooking of specific foods that represented the harvest, especially porridge and bread, often with fresh seasonal fruit being incorporated (Danaher, 1972). There is also mention of cows being milked in the morning and the milk used in the feast, as well as a special type of bread being made from harvested grain and cooked with rowan or another sacred wood before being handed out by the head of the household to the family who eats it and then walks sun-wise around the cooking fire, chanting a blessing prayer (McNeill, 1959). It was understood that the period just prior to the beginning of the harvest was the leanest of the year, making the celebration of fresh fruit, vegetables, and grains all the more special to the people (MacNeill, 1962). This may also be symbolically related to another legend of Lughnasa, the battle between the God Lugh and the mysterious mythic figure of Crom Dubh. Crom Dubh means the 'black bent one' and he had a special day on the last Sunday of July called Domhnach Crom Dubh and a dangerous bull bent on destruction that had to be stopped to preserve the harvest (Kondratiev, 1998). Many of the myths relating to Lugh and Crom Dubh, who is sometimes called Crom Cruach, involve Lugh battling and outwitting Crom and thus insuring the safety and bounty of the harvest; in some cases this theme is given the additional layer of the defeat, sacrifice, consumption, and then resurrection of Crom's bull, which may argue for an older element of bull sacrifice on this day (MacNeill, 1962). The Carmina Gadelica records several specific actions and charms to be done during the first harvest which expand on the importance of this turning point of the year.

Another common practice at Lughnasa was for people to gather together outdoors at a traditional place, often with the entire community getting together, and the site chosen would not only be someplace beautiful and wild but remote enough that traveling to it would represent something of a challenge (Danaher, 1972). Other practices of Lughnasa include decorating holy wells and pillar stones on this date, and also of traveling to hill or mountaintops; all of these varied by location and indicate that while the festival itself was widespread the nature of the celebration was dependent on the area and took on a unique local flavor (MacNeill, 1962). There are references to blessing cattle on the eve of Lughnasa and of making blessing charms for the cattle and milking equipment that the blessing would remain for the year to come (McNeill, 1959). Divination was practiced, with a particular focus on the weather during the harvest, and this seems to have been based on observations of the weather so far during the year and on atmospheric conditions on Lughnasa, with color and appearance of certain landmarks indicating either fair or foul weather to come (Danaher, 1972). Lughnasa was also the time in Ireland, Scotland, and the Orkneys for handfastings and weddings, or the dissolution of unions formed in the previous year (McNeill, 1959). Trial marriages of this type were used to see if the new couple was compatible; should they choose to separate after a year there was no shame in it and any child that was produced from the union would be ranked with the father's legal heirs (McNeill, 1959). Finally Lughnasa was also well known for harvest fairs and an assortment of athletic competitions and horse races; it is important to note that the ancient fairs, or oenacha, were not occasions of commerce but of social gathering and celebration (MacNeill, 1962). Many different types of games were held, as well as competitions of agility and strength, fire leaping, and swimming races of both men and horses (Danaher, 1972). A general party atmosphere prevailed with dancing and music, storytelling, feasting, and bonfires (Evert-Hopman, 2008). Overall it can be gathered from a wide understanding of the various Lughnasa customs that this celebration was one based on the gathering together of the community to celebrate the fresh abundance of a new harvest with joy and enjoyment. People gathered to reinforce and celebrate the bonds of community through marriages and social mixing, and to strengthen and honor the bonds between the people and the spirits of the land and the Gods through decorating wells and holy stones, the re-telling or re-enactment of mythological tales, acts of blessing, and ritual.

It is unknown now exactly what pagan religious ceremonies may have been held on Lughnasa, but there are several deities that we do know are associated with this holy day. The most obvious deity associated with Lughnasa is of course Lugh, who battles with Crom Dubh and is also said to have instituted the games to commemorate his foster mother. Tailtiu herself could be another deity associated with Lunasa, as could the Goddess Áine who in some mythology is connected to both a three-day period during Lughnasa and to the mythic figure of Crom Dubh as his consort during this time (MacNeill, 1962). Another Goddess associated with Lughnasa is Macha, one of the Morrignae, who some believe raced the king's horses on Lughnasa; whether or not this is so there is evidence of a longstanding celebration of Lughnasa at Emain Macha and the surrounding areas in Ulster (MacNeill, 1962). The harvest itself may also be connected to the Cailleach, as it was a common custom to associate the last sheaf in the field with the Cailleach. However, this may be more appropriate later in the harvest season at Harvest Home or Samhain (Danaher, 1972).

We can see from all of this that Lughnasa is a complex and multi-faceted holiday with a rich history of traditions and practices. If you are really interested in learning more about it I highly recommend MacNeill's book The Festival of Lughnasa – at over 700 pages it is more than worth the cost.

It is clear from the history of the holiday that for a modern practitioner there is an abundance of material to work with in finding ways to celebrate Lughnasa. I'm going to offer several suggestions for practice that could be used for anyone with a Celtic leaning, or who would like to celebrate this holy day in a Celtic manner, but I leave the actual ritual up to the individual or group to design. My own approach to this holiday is Irish reconstructionist in nature and that doubtless colors my view, but I would like to offer this to anyone of any faith who celebrates Lughnasa.

One aspect that should be celebrated the same whether a person is solitary or in a group is food. Ideally if you grow your own fruit or grain, or have a milk cow, you could use the product of your own harvest, otherwise you should try to find high quality, local foods to use. Most Irish cookbooks should offer recipes for Barm Brac and you can substitute fresh fruits like raspberries and blackberries for the raisins and dried peel the recipe calls for. Although corn is often mentioned in relation to Lughnasa it is likely used to mean oats, and was replaced in time by potatoes as the main produce crop. It would be fine to use new world corn, especially if gluten sensitivity is an issue, if that is a local crop that is being harvested in your area at this time, or alternately to use wheat or oats to cook with. In the same way that there are many Barm Brac recipes to choose from there are innumerable porridge recipes to which fruit can be added, and fresh milk would also be appropriate. I would suggest leaving a portion of whatever is prepared out as an offering after the celebration, either to the daoine sidhe or the Gods you decide to honor, or to both.

If you are practicing with a group the group should choose a suitable place outdoors to meet, preferably either on a high place like a hilltop or mountain, or by the seashore or a river, or other place considered sacred by the group. Everyone should bring a small token dish to represent their contribution to the harvest, and if possible a fire should be kindled. The group should feel relaxed and social while setting up and getting comfortable stories should be told relating to Lughnasa; if possible music should be played or people can be encouraged to sing. It would also be alright to decorate a local stone, tree, or spring with flowers or other appropriate biodegradable decorations. At this point the group can celebrate the religious rite in whatever way they prefer, with the entire festivities dedicated to the God or Gods of the rite. The food should be reheated using the fire and then shared and eaten by all, with some left as an offering as previously mentioned; this can be done during the group's religious ritual or afterwards depending on the group. More stories can be told and music played while people socialize, and then the group should have whatever athletic games they are best able to hold. This could involve foot races, contests of strength, solving puzzles, or games of skill, like tossing a bean bag through a ring with the winner receiving a special token or prize. After the athletic games, if the fire has died down a bit, it would also be traditional for people to jump the fire. The celebration should be planned to last for the entire day and the tone should be fun and light hearted.

In contrast, a solitary practitioner may have to work a bit harder to include athletic aspects, or choose not to include them at all. I would suggest if you are alone that you choose a location to celebrate that will be physically challenging to get to, and include getting to and leaving the site as part of the athletic challenges of the day. You could hike to a high place or other sacred site and then, if it's safe, build a fire do so. Sitting alone you can recite stories, poetry, or sing while preparing the area; decorating a tree or other sacred object can be done alone. You can then celebrate your solitary rite as you choose, dedicating your efforts to the deity or deities you are honoring. In the same way when you bring out and eat the food you have brought be sure to leave some as an offering. You may choose to sit for a while in silence contemplating the beauty of your location or the meaning of the holy day, or you may find ways to challenge yourself (safely) to physical activities where you are. You can even jump the fire by yourself when it is low enough. Spend as much time as you would like at your ritual site, enjoying it, and then clean up and head home.

There are many traditions associated with Lughnasa that emphasize both community and connecting to the divine. Some of these traditions pass beyond recorded history and into supposition and guesswork, but many are firmly based in folk practices that continued well into the last century. By learning about and understanding the old traditions of Lughnasa we can find new ways to incorporate them into modern pagan practices, and doing so will deepen our own spirituality.

References:

Danaher, K., (1972). The Year in Ireland; Irish Calendar Customs
Evert-Hopman, E., (2008). A Druid's Herbal of Sacred Tree Medicine
Kondratiev, A., (1998). Apple Branch: a Path to Celtic Ritual
MacNeill, M., (1962). The Festival of Lughnasa
McNeill, F. M., (1959). The Silver Bough, volume 2: A Calendar of Scottish National Festivals, Candlemas to Harvest Home

A Personal Lughnasa

Tuesday, August 2, 2011

Well another Lughnasa has come and gone...

This year most of my plans for celebrating had to be cancelled due to illness, but I was able to have a nice quiet celebration yesterday with my family. We started off with a nice breakfast of oatmeal and raspberries we picked from our yard and then the girls and I spent the day together while my husband worked. We cleaned the ritual room and re-did the main altar while talking about what Lughnasa was to us. My three-year-old decided it was a time to honor the 'Goddess in the earth', while my seven-year-old described it as 'a really fun harvest time, that's hot, when we get to eat yummy food.' I told them stories from Irish mythology: the tale of Macha racing the kings horses, how Tailtiu cleared the plains, the story of when Lugh came to Tara... and we had our own sorts of athletic games, which were far more comical than athletic really, but were very fun nonetheless.

After my husband arrived back home from work there was music, although his style is far from traditional, and some more general cleaning and re-arranging, before dinner. The main course was roast chicken, fresh veggies from the local farmer's market and oat bread (from the bakery down the street) with honey. And after all that cooking and good food, the children's favorite part of the meal was the orange frosted sugar cookies we had for dessert. A plate was made up as an offering to the Gods and another for the daione sidhe and later on both were placed outside on the outdoor altar. The ritual itself was private and simple.

I'm left today reflecting on my own harvest this year, on the things that have gone according to plan and the things that have decidedly not. I always find that Lughnasa ends up being a period of introspection for me, perhaps because I don't have much of a physical harvest in terms of planting and reaping. As I see the world around me ripening and offering up its abundance to those able to recognize and collect it I can't help but look at the things in my own life that have changed since spring, good and bad, and about what I can harvest.

I also learned this year that I can find a way to celebrate a holiday under any circumstances.

Moon of Blessings

When I see the new moon,
It becomes me to lift my eyes
It becomes me to bend my knee
It becomes me to bow my head

Giving you praise, you moon of guidance,
That I have seen you again,
That I have seen the new moon,
The lovely leader of the way.

Many a one has passed beyond
In the time between the two moons,

Though I am still enjoying earth,
You moon of moons and of blessings!
The Silver Bough

There is no evidence that the Celts had a particular deity associated with the moon, as far as I have ever seen, but there are many little charms and prayers, like this one from McNeill's Silver Bough, volume 1, that praise the moon and its blessings. It was traditional in several areas of Scotland and the outer Islands to make certain gestures towards the new moon when it was first seen in the sky each month, as Carmichael notes in volume one of his work:

> *When they first see the new moon they make obeisance to it as a great chief. The women curtsey gracefully and the men bow low, raising their bonnets reverently. The bow of the men is peculiar, partaking somewhat of the curtsey of the women the left knee being bent and the right drawn forward towards the middle of the left leg in a curious but not awkward manner.*
>
> *In Cornwall the people nod to the new moon and turn silver in their pockets. In Edinburgh cultured men and women turn the rings on their fingers and make their wishes. A young English lady told the writer that she had always been in the habit of bowing to the new moon, till she had been bribed out of it by her father, a clergyman, putting money in her pocket lest her lunar worship should compromise him with his Bishop. She naively confessed, however, that among the free mountains of Loch Etive she reverted to the good customs of her fathers, from which she derived great satisfaction!* (Carmichael, pp 123-124, 1900)

Last night I spotted the first sliver of new moon, as the clouds cleared and then closed in again. I felt my heart lift to see that shining silver crescent hanging there, promising another month of moonlight and I said the prayer from the Silver Bough. I found myself feeling a sort of kinship with my ancestors who must have seen that light each month with the same feeling of promise, felt even more strongly since, without electric lights, they would have relied on the moon far more than we do today. So I prayed and spun my rings on my fingers and I thought about the power of these little things to make me feel connected to my spirituality and to my ancestors. Every month I find myself searching the sky for the new moon until I see it and when I do my heart always lifts at the sight and a little prayer falls from lips, almost of its own accord.

When people think of bringing back or reconstructing the old pagan ways of different cultures many seem to go automatically to the big things, the seasonal rites, worshipping the Gods, rites of passage, but it is the little things, the daily things, that really matter the most because these are the backbone of living the faith, I think.

References:

Carmichael, M., (1900). Carmina Gadelica. Retrieved from http://www.sacred-texts.com/neu/celt/cg1/cg1057.htm

McNeill, F., (1956). The Silver Bough, volume 1

New Moon Prayer 2

This is my own personal practice whenever I see the new moon for the first time each month, something I have done for a long time, although the prayer changes; sometimes it is spontaneous poetry, or even silence, while others I might recite some traditional prayer as in this example.

At my first glimpse of the new moon in the sky the other night I kissed my fist, saluted the moon with it, and recited this prayer:

If you have found us
Well tonight, O Moon,
May your light leave us

Seven times still more blessed
O Moon so fair,
May it be so,
As seasons come,
And seasons go.[5]

Sample Ritual for the Ocean

There is a considerable amount of material within the Celtic cultures that lends itself to modern ritual use. I'm including this example as a way to show how such material can be adapted and also, hopefully, inspire readers to do the same for themselves. This ritual was originally designed and written for the Gulf oil spill, and then distributed through Circle magazine and recommended for use after the Japanese nuclear disaster; it can also be used at any point for the healing of the ocean. It is meant for use by anyone of any tradition.

Ritual for Healing the Ocean Waters

Go to a source of running water, if possible, and hold ritual as you normally would. If you can't physically go to any water then decorate your altar with a water theme using whatever most connects you to the ocean. It may be best to invoke a sea or oceanic Deity, or focus on energy that resonates with the ocean. At the centerpoint of the ceremony make an offering to the water symbolic of healing, something safe and biodegradable; if you are inside use a bowl of water to represent the living water and place your offering in there. Say the following prayers:

O gods of the sea,
put health in the drawing waves,
to enrich the vast ocean,
to liven the dying waters.[6]

Make your offering. Then say:

I come here in prayer on this day,
Day to send healing on the vast waters,
Day to send health to fish and fowl,
Day to put right the web in the warp.

Day to put life in the briny waters,
Day to place health back in the ocean,
Day to cleanse, day to bless,
Day to put right a great wrong.

Day to put life back in the tide,
Day to send health to the life in the sea,
Day to make a most effective prayer,
Day of power, Gods bless the vast ocean,
Day of power, may the ocean be blessed.[7]

Finish ritual as you normally would. If you were indoors try to take the offerings to a source of water to pour them out so that they can symbolically be given to the ocean, while visualizing the water flowing into rivers, lakes, streams, larger rivers, and eventually the ocean herself, and your healing energy going where it needs to go.

Chapter 4

Honoring Life Passages

One aspect of modern practice that seems to be seeing an increase in popularity is the celebration of rites of passage. This is also an area that we have very little firm historic precedent for. Personally I see great value in using ritual and religion to honor the transition from one phase of life to another, especially in our modern world. I have researched different aspects of these rites and ways that they can be done in a Celtic format or ways that existing Celtic material can be adapted; the Carmina Gadelica is especially useful in this area.

In the following section I try to touch on some major areas where rites of passage can be applied, excluding only marriage. Historically marriage in Celtic countries seems to have been a simple affair based on publically pledging to each other, which resulted in complex legal ties between families. In a modern context this lends itself to a wide array of possibilities and allows each couple some flexibility, depending on how simple or complicated they want the ceremony to be. There are many books on the market that aim to help a couple plan and design their wedding and those books are a far better resource on the subject than I can be.

Irish Pregnancy Folklore

Pregnancy in Irish folklore is an interesting topic and one that there does not seem to be a lot of available material on. There is a plethora of available material on birth, but pregnancy itself seems to be less often discussed. While I have not yet found much on actual practices relating to pregnancy there is some material to be found relating to folklore and superstitions about it.

Pregnancy was strongly emphasized in old Irish culture with a trial marriage only becoming permanent if a child was produced, and several of the Brehon laws addressing conception. For example there were laws that allowed either partner to sue for divorce due to the infertility of the other partner, or in the same situation for a temporary separation of the couple in order for the fertile partner to have a child with another person (Bital, 1996). Nonetheless I could find very little information relating to pregnancy folklore or folk practices besides those relating to conception and birth. The actual pregnancy itself is rarely discussed in sources.

What I did find out was that there is a small selection of Irish superstitions relating to pregnancy. It was thought that if a pregnant woman saw a hare run across her path her child would be born with a cleft lip unless she ripped the hem of her dress or skirt (O hÓgain, 1995; O Suilleabhain, 1967). Similarly if a pregnant woman twisted her foot in a graveyard her child would be born with a twisted foot (O Suilleabhain, 1967). A pregnant woman should never help prepare a corpse or attend a wake, for fear of a similar fate befalling her unborn child (O hÓgain, 1995; O Suilleabhain, 1967). Nor should an expectant mother attend a bride, although a pregnant woman was thought to be especially lucky for a blacksmith's forge and might be asked to grant that luck to the smith by pumping the bellows (O Suilleabhain, 1967). Generally it seems that the belief was that an unborn baby was easily influenced by outside circumstances and powers and so needed special protections from interference.

In contrast there are a multitude of beliefs and practices relating to the birth itself. These include things like inviting the Goddess (or saint) Brighid in while the woman is laboring and untying all knots within the birth room, including unbraiding the mother's hair, to symbolically open the way for the baby.

This at least forms a very basic idea of some of the popular beliefs about pregnancy in Ireland. As a modern polytheist I might make use of this information by using extra protections and prayers for my child's health and safety. I have also personally avoided any in-depth spiritual journey work or any other intense spiritual work during pregnancy. This information would also support a type of baby shower that emphasizes blessing and well wishes for the unborn child, perhaps with each guest bringing something symbolic of the blessing they want to impart.

References:

O hÓgain, D., (1995). Irish Superstitions
O Suilleabhain, S., (1967). Nosanna agus Piseoga ne nGeal
Bitel, L., (1996). Land of Women

A Baby Blessing

The child should be dressed in something beautiful and meaningful for the family. If indoors, a small altar can be created with a candle (triple wicked if possible) and a bowl of sacred water, as well as something representing a tree. These symbolize the three Celtic realms of land, sea, and sky that form the bedrock of our world and were used to swear oaths in ancient times. If outdoors, the altar should be prepared in front of a tree and contain the candle and water. The officiant should walk three times sunwise around the altar holding the infant and chanting:

Once for Danu, mother of the people of peace,
We go around the path of the sun, beloved one

Once for Lugh, many skilled God,
We go around the path of the sun, beloved one

Once for those who have gone before,
We go around the path of the sun, beloved one

To aid you from the Fairy-kin
To guard you from the Host

To aid you from the Fairy-hound
To shield you from the specter

To keep you under the mantle of the Gods
To shield you, to surround you,

To save you from powers that threaten
To fill you with blessed imbas[8]

Three times round we go
To wash you in inspiration.

The child should then be passed (with extreme care!) over the candle flame to the father, back across the flame to the officiant, and then across a third time back to the mother. (If the infant is wearing anything long or flowing I would put the candle on the ground for this part to ensure maximum safety.) The officiant should then pick up the bowl of water and, dipping their fingers in, should drip water onto the child's forehead for each line of the following:

A little wave for your form,
A little wave for your voice,
A little wave for your sweet speech.

A little wave for your means,
A little wave for your generosity,
A little wave for your appetite.

A little wave for your wealth,
A little wave for your life,

A little wave for your health.

Nine little waves for you
By land, sea, and sky
In the names of the Gods of my people,
The spirits of the Otherworld,
And the ancestors whose blood lives within you.

The remaining water should be poured out at the roots of a tree, and the gathered family and well-wishers should feast and celebrate.

This ritual is based on material from the Carmina Gadelica volume 3 by Alexander Carmichael, adapted and paganized. The ritual is used by the Druid Order of the White Oak and may be used by anyone as desired.

Modern Rites of Passage for Young Adults

I'm a big believer in the importance of rites of passage to help anchor us in our spirituality and our sense of self. It's a very tribal way to do things, I think, to commemorate life changes with ritual. I know not everyone agrees or sees the need but for those who do...

I divided these up into girl and boy rituals, but there is flexibility in either to be reworked for the other gender, or for teens that identify with the other gender. I fully intend to use the first one for girls when my daughters are old enough – unless they'd rather go on a hunt.

Rite of Passage for a Girl

This first ritual is a rite of passage for a girl entering adulthood. Personally I would suggest doing it at the onset of menses, or roughly around 12 or 13. It is based on the Invocation of the Graces #3 from the Carmina Gadelica. Before the ritual the girl should have to face a challenge; this may include solving a riddle, making something by hand that challenges her skill, or finding something hidden. The exact challenge should be tailored to the girl, and should be difficult but not impossible.

Prepare the altar and ritual space as usual; place a bowl of sacred water on the altar. Process to the space and call on the ancestors, spirits of the land, and the Gods to witness the ritual. The assembled people should form a rough circle around the altar, while the officiant and girl stand before the altar. The officiant should ask the girl her name, why she has come before the assembly, and if she is ready to assume her new role within the community. The girl should answer honestly and from her heart to all the questions, present proof that she has passed her challenge, and if she is ready to proceed, the officiant should pick up the bowl of water and lightly wash her hands while reciting:

I wash your palms
In showers of wine,
In the lustral fire,
In the three elements,
In the juice of the rasps,
In the milk of honey.

Then the officiant should drip the sacred water on the girl's head, one drop for each line of the following, as it is recited:

I place the nine pure choice graces
In your fair fond face,
The grace of form,
The grace of voice,
The grace of fortune,
The grace of goodness,
The grace of wisdom,
The grace of generosity,
The grace of choice honor,

The grace of whole-souled loveliness,
The grace of goodly speech.

At this point the officiant should put the bowl of water down and stand with their hands on the girl's shoulders while saying:

Dark is yonder town,
Dark are those therein,
You are the young brown swan,
Going in among them.
Their hearts are under your control,
Their tongues are beneath your foot,
Nor will they ever utter a word
To give offence to you.
You are shade in the heat,
You are shelter in the cold,
You are eyes to the blind,
You are a staff to the traveler,
You are an island at sea,
You are a fortress on land,
You are a well in the desert,
You are health to the ailing.
Yours is the skill of the Fairy Woman,
Yours is the virtue of Brighid the calm,
Yours is the generosity of Danu, ever-flowing,
Yours is the bounty of Boann the fair,
Yours is the beauty of Emir the lovely,
Yours is the tenderness of Airmed, the gentle,
Yours is the courage of Macha the strong,
Yours is the charm of Fand of the wave.
You are the joy of all joyous things,
You are the light of the beam of the sun,
You are the door of the chief of hospitality,
You are the surpassing star of guidance,

You are the step of the deer of the hill,
You are the step of the steed of the plain,
You are the grace of the swan of swimming,
You are the loveliness of all lovely desires.
The best hour of the day be yours,
The best day of the week be yours,
The best week of the year be yours,
The best year in the lifetimes of men be yours.
Dagda has come and Ogma has come,
Brighid has come and Áine has come,
Boann and Manannan Mac Lir have come,
Lugh the many skilled has come,
Angus mac Og the beauty of the young has come,
Morrighan of the augury has come,
Dian Cecht, gifted God of healing has come,
And Miach the skilled healer of the host has come,
And Airmed the mild has come,
And the Spirit of true guidance has come,
And Danu, mother of the people of skill has come,
To bestow on you their affection and their love,
To bestow on you their affection and their love.

Afterwards the girl should thank the Gods, spirits, and ancestors and should make offerings to them. The ritual should be concluded in the normal manner and then the assembled people should celebrate with feasting and gift giving to the girl.

Rite of Passage for a Boy

This second ritual is a rite of passage for a boy entering adulthood. Personally I would suggest doing it roughly around 12 or 13, but it is up to the parents to decide when the boy is ready. It is based on Blessing the Hunter #114 from the Carmina Gadelica. This prayer was said as a consecration over a hunter before he went out to hunt. A very specific ritual was followed where he was anointed with oil while standing with his feet apart, each foot on a patch of bare ground, then handed a bow (Carmichael, 1900). Much like the blessing of a king or judge, this blessing came with specific prohibitions that acted as geas for the hunter throughout his life, usually relating to what animals he could and could not hunt. Specifically nursing or brooding animals were prohibited, as were unweaned or unfledged ones, and resting animals (Carmichael, 1900).

I would recommend that as part of the ritual, if possible, the boy actually participate in a hunt, either literally hunting and killing an animal or else a hunt that relies on skill, perhaps to retrieve a number of hidden items to prove himself. At the start of the ritual he may present the result of his hunt or the items that he found as proof of his success.

Prepare the altar and ritual space as usual; place oil for anointing the boy and a weapon, either real and to be used in the actual hunt, or symbolic, on the altar. Process to the space and call on the ancestors, spirits of the land, and the Gods to witness the ritual. The assembled people should form a rough circle around the altar, while the officiant and boy stand before the altar. The officiant should ask the boy his name, why he has come before the assembly, and if he is ready to assume his new role within the community. The boy should answer honestly and from his heart to all the questions and present proof of his success at completing his hunt, and if he is ready to proceed, the officiant should pick up the oil and anoint the boy's head while reciting:

You are the product of your ancestors,
May you be guided in the way that is right,
In the names of the Spirits of sea, earth and sky,
In name of the Gods of Life who bless you.
In the names of Ogma, and Nuada
Manannan of the wave, and Daghda the Good God,

Dian Cecht the healer, and Giobnui the smith
Macha the red, and Danu the mother of the aos sidhe.
In name of Lugh the many-skilled,
And Boann of the river,
Angus beloved, and sovereign Eriu,
Tailtiu calm, and Brighid of the milk and cattle.
In the name of Morrighan Goddess of hosts,
In the name of Anu, giver of abundance,
In the name of Flidias of the woodland glens,
And Airmed of the healing herbs.

The officiant should put down the oil and pick up the weapon, handing it to the boy with proper ceremony. When the boy takes it the officiant should continue, saying:

Until the time you shall have closed your eyes,
You shall not bend your knee nor move,
You shall not wound the duck that is swimming,
Never shall you harry her or her young.
The white swan of the sweet gurgle,
The speckled dun of the brown tuft,
You shall not cut a feather from their backs,
Till the world ends, on the crest of the wave.
They must be on the wing
Before you place missile to your ear,
And the fair Danu will give you of her love,
And the lovely Brighid will give you of her blessing.
You shall not eat fallen fish nor fallen flesh,
Nor one bird that was not brought down by skill,
Be thankful for the one,
Though nine should be swimming.
The fairy swan of Brighid of flocks,
The fairy duck of Danu of the people of peace.

Afterwards the boy should thank the Gods, spirits, and ancestors and should make offerings to them. The ritual should be concluded in the normal manner and then the assembled people should celebrate with feasting and gift giving to the boy. If an actual hunt was held then at the feast the assembled people can eat what the boy caught.

References:

Carmichael, A., (1900). Carmina Gadelica volume 1
Daimler. M., (2010). By Land, Sea, and Sky

A Modern Celtic House Blessing

Monday, December 5, 2011

Yesterday, I went out to a friend's new house (at their request) to cleanse and bless the space. It occurs to me that this sort of simple thing would be good for anyone to do themselves, either when moving in to a new home or perhaps once a year to bless the space. This method is entirely my own, as far as I know, and thoroughly modern, but is based on older methods and concepts.

First I walked through the house, room by room, burning herbs associated with cleansing. In general I recommend using a combination of vervain, rosemary, and juniper when possible, but any one of those alone is also good and the readily available sage bundles are also an option. Using smoke to purify and bless spaces and the home is an old Celtic practice, particularly using juniper. F. Marian McNeill in the Silver Bough says:

> *Juniper, or the mountain yew, was burned by the Highlanders both in the house and in the byre as a purification rite on New Year's morning' and the Gadelica itself says, 'Iubhar beinne [juniper] and caorran, mountain ash or rowan, were burnt on the doorstep of the byre on the first day of the quarter, on Beltaine Day and Hallowmas.'*

Likewise rosemary also has a strong historical association with cleansing, as according to Grieve's Modern Herbal it was burned to cleanse a sick room and was also believed to remove any evil influences in general (Grieve, 1931). Vervain was considered a sacred herb and used as an offering to the Gods in both the Celtic and Roman world.

Next I lit a white candle and walked through each room again praying for blessing on the home. This is based on traditions associated with certain holidays, like Samhain, where fire – usually in the form of a burning torch – would be taken around the boundary of a property to bless it and protect it.

In the end I stood in the middle of what would be the living room, holding the candle, and recited a prayer modified from the Carmina Gadelica:

Gods bless this house,
From site to stay,
From beam to wall,
From end to end,
From ridge to basement,
From balk to roof,
From foundation to summit,
Foundation and summit.

The above prayer is my own adapted version, it is changed very little from the original which can be found in the first volume of the Carmina Gadelica by Carmichael at the webpage http://www.sacred-texts.com/neu/celt/cg1/cg1048.htm

House Blessing 45

God bless the house,
From site to stay,
From beam to wall,
From end to end,

From ridge to basement,
From balk to roof-tree,
From found to summit,
Found and summit.

References:

McNeill, F., (1962). The Silver Bough
Carmichael, A., (1900). Carmina Gadelica
Grieve, M., (1931). A Modern Herbal
Daimler, M., (2012). By Land, Sea, and Sky

Prayer Upon Death

This is a blessing to be said at death. This could work equally well as something said to a dying person as they pass or as something said to those who are grieving during a funeral or memorial service.

Since we know the soul is immortal –
At the time of yielding the life,
At the time of pouring the sweat,
At the time of offering the life,
At the time of shedding the blood,
At the time of balancing the beam,
At the time of severing the breath,
At the time of loosing the soul,
Peace upon the soul's journey;
As it returns to the land from whence it came,
Peace upon the soul's journey,
As it returns from whence it came.
And may Mannanan, gentle and kindly,
Lord of the waves and guide across worlds,
Take possession of the beloved soul,
And shield it home,
Oh! Where it may rest and be reborn again.

Chapter 5

Celtic Magic

Celtic Folk Magic – Food

It's pretty much common knowledge among my friends and acquaintances that I have a strong interest in folk magic, both Irish and Celtic, although I also study other types like pow-wow and hoodoo (I'm not sure I'd categorize seidhr as folk magic). My interest is not purely academic; while I am interested in it from that perspective as well, my main focus is learning how to use it, both the traditional material and creating new charms that are in the same spirit. I have found the Carmina Gadelica to be a treasure trove of Celtic folk magic charms and also a wonderful way to learn more about the theory and approach that makes Celtic folk magic uniquely Celtic. Obviously for my purposes the Carmina Gadelica is overly Christian and so I end up adapting the material by removing the current deity references and replacing them with ones more fitting to my own approach, although there is an abundance of material that is useable as is. I am also comfortable creating new material that I feel is in the same spirit of traditional Celtic folk magic and I am going to include an example here .

One of the things that I like the most about the Celtic approach to folk magic is that it encompasses every aspect of daily living. There are few activities that seem exempt from the inclusion of a charm or ritual song and that really appeals to me. One of the ways that I do this is with food – I sing a little charm whenever I am mixing anything I am cooking, even something as simple as making Kool-aide. Food is a basic need, something we all depend on for survival, and something that we can easily add a blessing and good word to while it's being prepared. I stir deiseal, clockwise with the sun, the direction of blessing, focusing loving energy and thoughts of abundance and good health through the spoon and into the mix and sing something simple along the lines of:

I bless this food with love and health
Round with the moon, round with the sun
I bless this food with all good things
Round with the moon, round with the sun

It's easy to do, it's fun for my children, and I firmly believe that it adds something good to everything we eat. And I think it is in the spirit of traditional Celtic folk magic, even though the words and actions are new.

Celtic Healing Magic

Celtic healing magic, like all Celtic folk magic, relies on some basic principles: use of objects, both natural and manmade, transferring the spirit of one thing – in this case the illness – into nature, and the power inherent in certain items. By understanding these principles and how to apply them in different situations a person may effectively use folk magic healing in a Celtic style whenever there is a need for it.

Many types of Celtic folk healing rely on the use of objects and these fall into two categories: manmade and natural. In many spoken charms a metal knife, pin or other sharp object is used to threaten the afflicted area with the belief that this action will drive out the spirit that is the source of the affliction; there are several examples of this in the Carmina Gadelica. Another example of a manmade object used in healing is the brat Bhride, or Bride's Mantle, a piece of cloth that is left out on Imbolc eve with the belief that the Goddess Brighid (or Saint Brigit) will pass by in the night and touch the mantle, imparting some of her healing power to it. The Mantle can then be used throughout the year for healing people or animals by placing it over them, generally over their head. The Mantle is recharged each year on Imbolc by being left out; some believe the Mantle attains full power after seven years, while others say that after seven years it should be destroyed and a new Mantle created. In Scotland there is also the use of different colored thread for healing purposes. For example, red thread was worn during childbirth, and was worn with amber beads for protection. As well, rowan twigs were formed into a solar cross and wrapped with red thread for protection, especially of the home. Blue thread was worn as a charm against fevers, particularly in nursing mothers, and often these threads were passed down through a family. Black thread was tied with nine knots and worn as a cure for a sprain, something that could easily be combined with any of the spoken charms for sprains.

Natural objects were also commonly used for healing purposes. One common type of item thought to have healing powers was herbs, but not taken as a medicine, rather worn on the body, often by being sown into the clothes. Several of the healing charms in the Carmina Gadelica refer to this practice, but the herb was believed to work only if no one else knew you were wearing it. In addition there were very specific ways the herb must be gathered, generally before breakfast and without intent – meaning that you could not go out meaning to find that particular herb, but must find it as a lucky accident. All herbs gathered on Beltane have great power for good or ill, but they must not be pulled or broken by hand so the folklore discusses several means of gathering the herbs safely, such as tying a string to the herb and a dog so that the dog is the one to pull up the herb, or else putting your right hand out through your left sleeve and then pulling it back through your garment. Lady Wilde lists seven herbs of great value in her book, and these are: ground ivy, vervain, eyebright, groudsel, foxglove, the bark of the elder tree, and the young shoots of the hawthorn. Additionally, several sources list yarrow as the most powerful healing herb for any purpose.

Often any charm that used an object would also involve a spoken component, either a prayer or a spoken charm. I'm including a variety of examples. The words of the charm were combined with the proper action to achieve the desired result.

From Irish Cures and Superstitions by Lady Wilde

To Cure a Fever

Place the patient on the sandy shore when the tide is coming in, and the retreating waves will carry away the disease. (In modern practice you could visualize this or create a chant using this imagery.)

For Hip Disease

Take three green stones, gathered from a running brook, between midnight and morning while no word is said. In silence it must be done. Then uncover the limb and rub each stone several times closely downwards from hip to toe, saying:

Wear away, wear away
There you shall not stay
Cruel pain, away, away.

A Very Ancient Charm Against Wounds or Poisons

Hold your hands over the wound or affected area and chant:

The poison of a serpent, the venom of the dog,
The sharpness of spear, does not do well in man.
The blood of one dog, the blood of many dogs,
The blood of the hound of Fliethas – these I invoke.
It is not a wart to which my spittle is applied.
I strike disease; I strike wounds.
I strike the disease of the dog that bites,

Of the thorn that wounds
Of the iron that strikes.
I invoke the three daughters of Fleithas
Against the serpent
Benediction on this body to be healed;
Benediction on the spittle;
Benediction on him who casts out disease.

From Scottish Charms and Amulets by George Fraser Black

To Bless Water with a Healing Crystal

Dip the healing crystal in the water while saying:

Let me dip you in the water
You beautiful gem of power
In water of purest wave
Which Bridget kept pure
A blessing on the gem
A blessing on the water and
A healing of bodily ailments
To each suffering creature.

From the Carmina Gadelica Volume 2 by Alexander Carmichael

Charm for the Rose [Mastitis] 124

Thou rose deathly, deadly, swollen,
Leave the udder of the white-footed cow,
Leave the udder of the spotted cow,
Leave, leave that swelling,
And betake thyself to other swelling.
Thou rose thrawn, obstinate,
Surly in the udder of the cow,

Leave thou the swelling and the udder,
Flee to the bottom of the stone.
I place the rose to the stone,
I place the stone to the earth,
I place milk in the udder,
I place substance in the kidney.

Tooth Charm 126

The incantation put by lovely Bride
Before the thumb of the Mother of God,
On lint, on wort, on hemp,
For worm, for venom, for teeth.
The worm that tortured me,
In the teeth of my head,
Hell hard by my teeth,
The teeth of hell distressing me.

The teeth of hell close to me;
As long as I myself shall last
May my teeth last in my head.

Variants

On lint, on comb, on agony.
On sea, on ocean, on coast.
On water, on lakes, on marshes

Charm for a Sprain 130

Bride went out
In the morning early,
With a pair of horses;
One broke his leg,
With much ado,
That was apart,
She put bone to bone,

She put flesh to flesh,
She put sinew to sinew,
She put vein to vein;
As she healed that
May I heal this.

From By Land, Sea, and Sky by Morgan Daimler

Charm for Mastitis

When performing these charms a sharp object such as a knife or pin should be held towards the body part, you should spit on your fingers and trace a triskele on the area while invoking land, sea, and sky. This follows a common method of folk healing where the illness or injury is threatened as if it were a sentient thing, and ordered to leave the person it is tormenting. All healing charms would be recommended in addition to traditional and alternative medical treatments for the conditions.

Charm 122

See, Blessed Brighid
The breast of this mother is swollen:
May you give peace to this breast
May you subdue the swelling;

May you give peace to this breast
May you subdue the swelling.
I see it myself, Brighid,
The suffering of this mother
May you appease this breast,
May you subdue the swelling;

May you appease this breast,
May you subdue the swelling.
See, Healing Goddess

Midwife of all mothers,

May you appease this breast,
May you subdue the swelling;
May you appease this breast,
May you subdue the swelling
Brighid sees the suffering
And she does what is needed
She gives ease to the breast
And rest to the swelling;
She gives ease to the breast
And rest to the swelling.

Charm for a Toothache 126

The incantation put by Brighid
Before the Mother of the Gods,
On sea, on ocean, on coast.
For painful aching teeth.
The pain that tortured me,
In these teeth in my head,
Agony hard with my teeth,
This agony distressing me.
I put this pain far from me;
As long as I myself shall last
May my teeth last in my head.

To Remove Blood from Urine 180

By the tides of the eternal sea,
By the bedrock of the firm earth,
By the ceaseless winds of sky,
So shall this be.
Great wave, red wave,
Strength of sea, strength of ocean
The nine wells of Mac Lyr

To pour help on you
Put a stop to the blood,
Put a flood to the urine.

Charm for Tumors

I've used this charm before for cancer patients with success, and so have chosen to include it here. It is a heavily rewritten version of a pow-wow chant; I would recommend the book Pow-wows, or Long Lost Friend for more on this school of folk magic.

The charm should be chanted while holding your hands over the afflicted area, or a picture of the person. I highly recommend doing this charm on a set regular basis, for example three times a day for a series of nine or 27 days. In order for the charm to be effective it must be done often and consistently.

A Charm to Reduce and Heal Tumors

Nine waves upon the ocean
The nine become eight,
The eight become seven,
The seven become six,
The six become five,
The five become four,
The four become three,
The three become two,
The two become one,
One becomes none;
Out from the marrow into the blood,
Out from the blood into the flesh,
Out from the flesh into the skin,
Out from the skin into the hair,
Out from the hair to the healing earth.

References:

Wilde, L., (1991). Irish Cures, Mystic Charms, and Superstitions

Fraser Black, G., (1898). Scottish Charms and Amulets
McNeill, F., (1959). The Silver Bough, volume 1
Carmichael, A., (1900) Carmina Gadelica
O hÓgain, D., (2006). Lore of Ireland

Oracular Practices and Magic – When Cultures Meet

I have been practicing various forms of trancework and magic for a very long time now but often using a more general learn-through-experimentation method, although I have always been interested in culture specific practices. The first ten years or so of my practice was entirely self taught, with the attending mishaps, experimentation, and misadventures. Around 1999 I was lucky enough to meet several people who had actually been trained in various methods and I learned a lot from them by association, but I still wanted to learn more traditional, particularly Irish, practices. The problem was that at that point I wasn't aware of anyone who was actively using them and I lacked the resources to really find out if anyone was reviving these methods and I was unsure how to do so myself. In 2006 or so when I started honoring the Norse Gods and Odin came calling, I became aware of the Norse practice of seidhr. Now right off the bat I could see the similarities between seidhr and the Irish practices which might have been grouped together and called fáidetóracht[9] (modern Irish fáidheadóireacht) although there may be a better word that encompasses all aspects from the prophecy to the active magic in the way that seidhr does for the Norse. I do know now that people are working to reconstruct these Irish methods, but so far what I have seen takes the poet's approach and that is not where my focus is. While I am something of a poet I do not follow the poet's path when it comes to magic, but rather take a more, shall we say, Druidic approach (we already know my opinion about the fluid nature of the different titles, Druid and poet).

So, anyway, in 2006 or so I began reading about seidhr and

soon after started putting what I read into practice with the help of several friends and friends-of-friends who also practiced and could offer practical advice. Again I was lucky not only to have knowledgeable people to go to with questions, but also because very shortly I had the members of my kindred showing an interest as well. While it was enormously intimidating to feel responsible for training them when I was literally only one step ahead in learning, it was a great motivator and provided a needed structure and safety. I have been doing public spae (oracular seidhr) sessions for several years now as well as regularly practicing with my own group and I am at a point when I really need to start transitioning what I know from seidhr into actively practicing the Irish methods. I have a real block about doing that, for some reason, but the only way to get around it is to just push through it I suppose.

We know from the available material that seidhr was something of an outsiders' practice, often equated in later material to witchcraft, and that men who practiced it were seen as being unmanly. Despite this there is evidence, such as the story of the Spaekona in Eric the Red's Saga, that people who practiced oracular seidhr, also called spae, travelled from village to village as guests to foretell the community's fate. As with many such practices there is some division of the 'good' and 'bad', or positive and destructive practices into two different categories with people who were generally seen as positive being called spae workers while those with darker reputations were known as seidhr workers. It seems to me that what each group actually did was very similar and it was only in the judgment of the outcome or who it was being done against that decided the label. According to Ynglinga Saga seidhrworkers were said to be able to control the weather by stilling the ocean or turning the wind, could put out fires, shapeshift by sending their spirit out in the form of an animal, could tell the future, could speak to the dead (a practice called utisetta or out-sitting) and could bring death, ill luck and illness, or life, good luck and health. The Voluspa mentions the seidhr worker's ability to influence the minds of other people and to use magic charms, and of course Eric the Red's Saga talks about spirit communication and telling the future.

In the Irish we see Druids having the power of prophecy, later described as being done through several methods called imbas forosnai, dichetal do chennaib and tenm laida, which were attributed to the poets, but seem to have been Druidic in nature to me as St. Patrick outlawed two of the three for calling on pagan Gods. The idea of extemporaneous prophecy appears in several Irish legends in which a Druid predicts a certain outcome of a day or event, or, as in the legend of Deirdre of the Sorrows, after touching someone or something, which are methods in line with the poetic methods. Druids are also able to either literally change shape with the fith fath or to make others perceive them in another shape, and also in the old stories have the power to influence the weather, call fog, as well as to affect people's health for good or ill.

References:

Chadwick, N., (1935) Imbas Forosnai. Retrieved from http://searchingforimbas.blogspot.com/p/imbas-forosnai-by-nora-k-chadwick.html

Blain, J., (2001). Nine Worlds of Seidhr MagicIrish and Norse mythology and folklore, especially the Saga of Eric the Red, Ynglinga Saga, Voluspa, the Cath Maige Tuired, the Tain Bo Cuiligne, and the stories of the Fianna.

Getting Seidhr-y with It

Firstly to clarify terms: seidhr is a Norse word with an uncertain meaning that is often translated as witchcraft, or less commonly as shamanism. (I favor the witchcraft translation although neither is really a good English descriptor for what seidhr work encompasses.) As I mentioned before, seidhr had something of a bad reputation so seidhr might also be called spa or spae (interestingly spae is actually the Scottish version of the word). There was a slight technical nuance between the two in terms of oracular work, as a spae worker gathered information in a manner strongly reminiscent of Celtic forms of divination like tenm laida or imbas forosnai while a seidhr worker called spirits to herself to answer questions (see the link to the Viking Answer Lady below for more on this). In terms of my own practice I do both, but I have a bad habit of using the term spae for all oracular work, even that which should technically be considered seidhr. Secondly both seidhr and spae involve practices that can be seen as manipulative of other people to various degrees. I am well aware of this and I am comfortable with my own ethics and take responsibility for my actions and the outcomes. I believe in the end all magic is neutral and it is through our own perception that it is judged as good or bad, and I'm okay with trusting my own judgment. Thirdly, yes I actually use these methods; this isn't just academic discussion for me. I have spent over a decade – nearly two at this point – learning and practicing these things. I truly believe in them, and I really do them.

Any type of seidhr work, to me, involves some level of trance work and so needs to be done carefully and with protection. That may mean different things for different people and groups; to me it means warding the space when doing deeper work, especially oracular work, and having allies to watch my back. I am dedicated to Odin, who knows seidhr work, and I have a shrine to Freya, who they say was the first to teach seidhr to the Aesir. Before any planned working I offer to them both, as well as to a certain obscure Germano-Celtic Goddess who took an interest in what I do (is anyone really surprised that when I started doing this I had a Germano-Celtic Goddess show up?) I offer to my ancestors and to other particular spirits I work with when doing this type of work. For less intense daily work I trust to my personal wards and protection. If you don't know what that is or how to do it then you aren't ready to be doing any of this type of trance work.

Now things like weather work and shapeshifting I generally do when I am alone; it was common in both traditional seidhr as well as some types of Irish magic like the tarbh feis for the person working to withdraw to a quiet place alone and lay or sit with their head covered. In seidhr work this is called going under the cloak and was also used by skalds (poets); it is a type of meditation that can be used for a variety of purposes from spellcasting, spirit journeying, to contacting spirits and for prophecies and poetic inspiration. I have found that even putting my hands over my eyes is effective for entering a trance. Influencing the weather is not my forte, although I've had success with it; it takes a lot of energy and concentration and is usually done in a lighter trance. It involves, for me, going to where I want the change to manifest and then visualizing that change for as long as I can. It is a very tiring thing to do though and I have only ever focused on very slight changes in localized areas. Calling storms is a seidhr practice that I have never done, although I have diverted the damage of a storm around my home. Shapeshifting can occur in any level of awareness, but I find I use it most often when my spirit is journeying outside my body, particularly when travelling in the Otherworld (hedge-witches call this 'crossing the hedge'). Such travelling, at least in human shape, seems to be common in modern seidhr, especially oracular work as many groups use a method where they journey to the gates of Hel or to the Well of Wyrd to answer questions. I haven't seen similar accounts in the lore, accept in the case of one story where a man sent his spirit in the form of a bear to fight against some other men – the bear disappeared when the man was awakened from his trance.

When alone or with my own group I tend to use this travelling method to go find answers. Now my personal preference for a public oracular method is different, based on what I have reconstructed from the story of the spae worker in Eric the Red's Saga. I sit in a seat before the gathered people, with my face covered,[10] and in my mind I recite a chant I have written to call any goodly inclined, helpful spirits to me to answer the questions that will be asked. This does involve going into a deeper trance and after the session I will not remember anything that was said, by myself or others, although so far the results have been very good. I do not personally use drumming, although I can and have worked with someone using drumming; it's just not something that I need. I am contemplating adding the use of a staff though, both to hold and to tap on the floor, so that might be the next experiment. Most of what I do at this point is the result of years of trial and error learning and it is still evolving as I learn new methods.

Another seidhr practice is called sjonhverfing, or 'deceiving of the sight'. This is roughly equivalent to Irish glamour or fith fath, where you make others see or perceive what you want them to instead of what is really there. An example of this type of seidhr magic is seen in Eyrbyggja Saga where a seidhr worker saves a man who is being chased by making the men chasing him see only a household object (a staff if I remember correctly) where the man is sitting. I have been doing this type of magic for far longer than any other of the skills listed under the auspices of seidhr, and of all the practices I think this one is the most directly similar between the Irish and Norse. You simply focus on the other person or people seeing what you want them to see, and act as if you are fully confident that they see it. The real trick for me is to pay attention and only do it when I want to, because it's very inconvenient to accidently influence things. And it is probably irresponsible, but nobody is perfect, and like anything else getting control of this is a matter of practice and time.

A final well known seidhr practice is utisetta, or sitting out. Utisetta is done to contact the spirits of the dead, by sitting out on a grave or mound wrapped in a cloak. As with the Irish tales of those who choose to sleep on a fairy mound, utisetta in the lore could be very dangerous, but could also offer many rewards, especially through new knowledge and prophecy, which the Norse believed could be given by the dead. I have used utisetta with the dead in a cemetery only once; generally I use it to contact the land vaettir and alfar (daione si by another name). It works perfectly well for that, and I suppose the way I do it is truly a synchretic practice as I am using a Norse method for a Celtic end...

References:

http://www.vikinganswerlady.com/seidhr.shtml
http://www.freyja.org/seidr.htm
http://www.hrafnar.org/seidh.html
http://www.sunnyway.com/fenvala/he_seidh.html
http://www.boudicca.de/seidhr-e.htm
Paxson, D., (2008). Trance-Portation
Blain, J., (1999). Nine Worlds of Seid Magic

Celtic Ways of Seeing

So now that we've covered some different aspects of seidhr historically and how I am trying to reconstruct and practice them, let's look at the Irish side of things. Now we know that there were some very specific methods used by the File during the transition period between paganism and Christianity because two of those methods were outlawed for calling on pagan Gods – which for our purposes is a good thing because it means that they were written about. There were three specific practices so written about and these were imbas forosnai – 'manifesting knowledge', tenm laida 'illumination of song', and dichetal do chennaib 'extemporaneous poetry' (Celtic Seers Sourcebook, 1999). Imbas forosnai involves preparing and eating meat (referenced as pig, cat, or dog specifically), making an offering to the Gods with specific chants and then lying down with the hands covering the eyes and sleeping or meditating for up to three days undisturbed to get certain knowledge or an answer. Another well known version of this may be the tarbh feis, which involves the sacrifice of a bull, eating its flesh and then wrapping up in its hide for the same purpose. Tenm laida seems to be, based on its appearance in myths, a type of light trance that a person could enter to answer specific questions, sometimes associated with touching the object directly and other times with putting the tips of your fingers or thumb in your mouth, such as in the stories of Finn mac Cool. In some stories it appears as a method to read the past or identify a body, although this also appears to be a type of seership practiced by both Scathach and Fidelm in mythology when answering questions about the future (Celtic Seers Sourcebook, 1999). Both of these methods were outlawed by the Christian Church for calling on 'idols'; the third method is dichetal do chenaib, which seems to resemble tenm laida but involves a deeper trance and the spontaneous speaking of poetry to answer the question. Perhaps the Prophecy of the Morrigan could be seen as this type of method. Dichetal do chenaib was not outlawed as it didn't directly call on pagan deities or spirits and was seen as a part of the poet's art.

Of these methods I see the most direct similarities to Norse practice in the imbas forosnai. The practice of retreating into a dark room, wrapped in a cloak to find inspiration – possibly a later version of imbas forosnai, I think – was seen in the Scottish Highlands until a few hundred years ago (Description of the Western Isles of Scotland, 1695). Interestingly during the conversion period in Iceland, when it looked like civil war was imminent, a leader used a similar method – laying down beneath his cloak – to find a compromise that would save the country. And in seidhr the seer is veiled when on the high seat.

Additionally we know that the ancient Celts, in general, used particular types of divination such as casting lots and a variety of omens including ornithomancy, or divination by observing the flight of birds. Ornithomancy was in fact so important that it continued in folk practice pretty much into the modern period with the Carmina Gadelica noting several omens that can be taken from the flight or call of certain birds. For example swans are considered very lucky, especially when seen flying, as it was believed that a swan was often an Otherworldly being in disguise, but to see or hear an owl, especially during the day, was considered unlucky (Carmina Gadelica, 1900). There is an excellent book called Birds of Ireland Facts, Folklore, and History by Glynn Anderson that includes a lot of the older folklore about each type of bird, which I have found invaluable for working up a system of bird omens to use. The Gadelica also discusses divination practices linked to the harvest, in which the harvesting tools were tossed in the air with how they landed indicating something about the fate of the person who owned the tool. The direction of the wind was also an omen, particularly on certain holy days (The Silver Bough, 1959).

One method of augury that is mentioned in enough detail to be used within the Gadelica is as follows:

The 'frith,'[11] *augury, was a species of divination enabling the 'frithir,' augurer, to see into the unseen. This divination was made to ascertain the position and condition of the absent and the lost, and was applied to man and beast. The augury was made on the first Monday of the quarter and immediately before sunrise. The augurer, fasting, and with bare feet, bare head, and closed eyes, went to the doorstep and placed a hand on each jamb. Mentally beseeching the God of the unseen to show him his quest and to grant him his augury, the augurer opened his eyes and looked steadfastly straight in front of him. From the nature and position of the objects within his sight, he drew his conclusions.*
(Carmina Gadelica, 1900).

The text is followed by a chant to be recited before opening the eyes; I have made my own version which is both more pagan and Irish deity specific. It is:

Gods over me, Gods under me
Gods before me, Gods behind me
I am on Your path, O Gods of life
and You are in my steps
The augury Morrighan made at the battle's end
The offering made of Brigid through Her palm
Did the spirits witness it?
The spirits did witness it.

The augury made by Morrighan about Her people
When the battle ended peace was made,
Knowledge of truth, not knowledge of falsehood,
That I shall see truly all my quest.

Kindly spirits and Gods of life,
May You give me eyes to see all I seek,
With sight that shall never fail, before me,
That shall never quench or dim.
(By Land, Sea, and Sky, 2010)

This is, of course, only a small fraction of the Celtic practices where omens and augury are concerned, but these represent specific areas that I am personally working on reconstructing or learning. I have had the most direct practice with tenm laida, as I understand it, and with working on learning omens and augury. I have used versions of the more modern style imbas forosnai, but have not yet tried the dichetal do chenaib. I feel more comfortable, in general, with the Norse divination methods, but I am trying to get more active with using what I know about the Celtic.

References:

A Description of the Western Isles of Scotland circa 1695
Daimler, M,. (2010). By Land, Sea, and Sky
Matthews, J., (1999). Celtic Seers Sourcebook
Carmichael, A., (1900). Carmina Gadelica
McNeill, F., (1959). The Silver Bough, volume 1

Irish Bird Omens

Ornithomancy, or taking omens from birds, has long been practiced by many cultures including the Celts. The lore and meanings associated with these omens have survived in modern cultural folklore surrounding birds, although it should be noted that such folklore is a living belief that is also influenced by other factors. Nonetheless for those interested in practicing modern ornithomancy, especially from a cultural perspective, such folklore is essential. In this section I am going to look at some Irish folklore surrounding birds that are also found in North America.

Ravens (Irish – Fiach Dubh)

One of the most well known birds of omen is the raven. Anytime ravens are in the area their activity, calls and direction of flight might be noted and interpreted, as they are generally seen as an ill omen. If a raven arrives just as a new task is being begun it is seen as an omen that the work will not end well, and a raven near a home signifies a death (O hÓgain, 1995). A raven hovering over a herd of livestock was thought to indicate disease among the stock, and to steal a raven's egg would result in the death of a human child (Anderson, 2008). On the other hand, should a raven with white on its wings fly to the right-hand side of a person and call out it was thought to be a sign of great luck for the person (Anderson, 2008).

Author Glynn Anderson suggests that most Irish lore about the raven is shared by the Norse and reflects Norse influence, which may be why the bird is seen simultaneously as a symbol of death and of wisdom, having been associated with Odin and used as symbols on the banners of different Vikings (Anderson, 2008). In Irish myth, ravens are associated with several deities including the Morrigan and Lugh. Ravens are seen as psychopomps who are able to travel between the world of the living and the world of the dead, as well as the Otherworld. They have strong associations as messengers, which may be why they are seen as such powerful birds of omen.

Crows (Irish – Feannóg)

Crows are seen with a similar mix of good and bad omens. It was believed that witches, fairies, bansidhe, and Badhbh appeared as hooded crows in Ireland, a belief that was especially strong in county Clare, and were thus seen as unlucky (Anderson, 2008). As with ravens, a crow landing on the roof of a house or flying over a home was an omen of death or disaster, but others believe that bad luck comes when crows leave an area (O hÓgain, 1995; Anderson, 2008).

Magpies (Irish – Snag Breac)

Magpies are thought to be the most unlucky bird to come across (O hÓgain, 1995). Also seen as omens of death, they were believed to be the souls of gossiping women; a magpie tapping on a window indicated a death and landing on a wagon (or car) indicated coming news of a death (Anderson, 2008). Because encountering a magpie was always unlucky different actions evolved to mitigate the bad luck, from taking off your hat and bowing to greeting the magpie and asking after its family, although turning around and returning home would also cancel any ill luck (Anderson, 2008). Only in County Mayo were magpies seen as lucky, and seeing a magpie was interpreted as a sign that good news was on its way (Anderson, 2008).

Cuckoo (Irish – Cuach)

Cuckoos were seen as omens of good weather (O hÓgain, 1995). To hear the first call of cuckoo in spring on the right-hand side foretold good luck all summer, but to hear it on the left meant difficult times ahead (Anderson, 2008; O hÓgain, 1995). To hear a cuckoo on your wedding day was lucky, but to hear it in the morning before breakfast indicated a lean year to come (Anderson, 2008). Where you first heard the cuckoo in the spring also had great meaning; in a graveyard it indicated a coming death, inside a building it meant bad luck, and the direction you were looking was where you would travel during the year (Anderson, 2008).

Swallow (Irish – Fáinleog)

Killing a swallow is seen to bring very bad luck, as is disturbing their nests; it's believed that the swallow can turn the cows' milk to blood (Anderson, 2008; O hÓgain, 1995). A swallow flying into your house was good luck, and if swallows built a nest in your barn it was sure to be safe from lightning; seeing a swallow while at sea was a good omen (Anderson, 2008). It was also believed that when you had your hair cut you should be careful in disposing of the clippings, because if a swallow lined her nest with them you would be afflicted with headaches the whole summer (Anderson, 2008).

Swan (Irish – Eala Bhalbh and Eala Ghlórach)

It was believed that swans were often actually Otherworldly beings or transformed people, so killing them was prohibited and to do so, even by accident, was very bad luck (O hÓgain, 1995; Anderson, 2008). While the feather of a swan was seen as a talisman of fidelity it was believed that the bodies of dead swans should not be touched (Anderson, 2008). In mythology swans were associated with the children of Lir who were cursed into that shape by their step-mother; in several myths deities and people of the sidhe assume the shapes of swans including Angus mac Og, Midhir, and Etain. Seeing a swan in flight was an omen of good luck, and one charm in the Carmina Gadelica invokes a swan to heal a child with the words: 'Leech of gladness thou/ Sain my little child/ Shield him from death/ Hasten him to health.' (Carmichael, 1900).

Robin (Irish – Spideog)

In New England robins are seen as signs of spring coming. In Ireland they represent a happy home, peace, and hope (Anderson, 2008). As such robins were never killed and if caught accidentally were always released; it was even believed once that cats would not kill robins (Anderson, 2008). Anyone who killed a robin would be afflicted with tremors or swollen hands and his cows would give blood with their milk (Anderson, 2008). Some say that the robin got his red breast by bringing fire to humanity (as did the swallow) while others attribute it to his aiding Jesus on the cross or bringing water into Hell to give to suffering souls (Anderson, 2008). When the first robin of spring was seen a wish could be made and as long as it was completed before the robin took flight it would come true (Anderson, 2008).

Robins may be associated with the God Bel/Bile/Belenos.

Wren (Irish – Dreoilín)

In the old traditions the wren and the robin were said to be married, and Anderson suggests that this may reflect an older belief that the two birds shared the year, with the wren representing darkness and winter while the robin symbolized light and summer (Anderson, 2008). The wren was a sacred bird to the Druids who sought omens from its song and saw wrens as messengers of the Gods; the Goddess Clíona was said to take the form of a wren (Anderson, 2008). Possibly due to this wrens were demonized by the church and hunted on Saint Stephen's Day, December 26th; although it may also relate to an older pagan practice of killing wrens at this time to symbolize the death of winter which they represented (Anderson, 2008). Since wrens were associated with winter and the Gods of winter I may see them as related to the Cailleach Bheur, although that is purely my own opinion. Oddly folk belief prohibits killing wrens or disturbing their nests at any other time of year (Anderson, 2008). The wren is said to be the king of the birds, after using cunning to win a contest among all the birds of Ireland; it was decided that whatever bird flew highest would be the king so the wren hid on the back of the eagle and at the height of the eagle's flight leaped up to win the crown.

Golden Eagle (Irish – Iolar Firean)

The golden eagle is one of the two types of eagle that were native to Ireland before being driven to extinction around a hundred years ago. Eagles were seen as symbols of wisdom, magical power, long life, speed, and vision (Anderson, 2008). In folklore some types of fairies, such as the Pooka, are said to appear at times in the shape of an eagle; personally I associate eagles with Nuada and Osprey with Manannan mac Lir. Additionally eagles appear often in Irish and more general Celtic mythology.

Hawk (Irish – Seabhac)

Ireland has an array of small hawks including the marsh hawk (croman na gcearc), goshawk (Clamhan), and sparrowhawk (Spiorog). Generally hawks were seen as messengers of the Otherworld, were connected to the willow, and believed to symbolize memory and 'clear sightedness' (Anderson, 2008). The oldest of all animals, according to myth, was the Hawk of Achill. It was believed that if hawks suddenly abandoned an area it was because an evil spirit was present (Anderson, 2008).

Owls (Irish – Ulchabhain)

The word for owl in Irish, ulchabhain, means 'bearded', although there are many associated folk names including cailleach oiche (night hag), screachan reilige (graveyard schreecher) and ceann cait (cat's head) (Anderson, 2008). Owls have often been associated with death and bad luck. Hearing an owl hoot, seeing one during the day, or having one fly across your path was seen as very unlucky, although throwing salt in the fire or turning one's clothes inside out should deflect the bad luck (Anderson, 2008). The methods for deferring the ill-omen are strongly reminiscent of methods to defend against fairies, so one might surmise a connection between these birds and the Good Neighbors.

Dove (Irish – Fearan)

Doves have long been viewed as symbols of peace and love. Irish folklore tells us that no ill-intentioned spirit can take the form of a dove (Anderson, 2008).

Heron (Irish – Corr Reisc)

Herons in folklore are often confused with cranes, as the name for them – corr reisc – means marsh crane. However, they are two distinct species (Anderson, 2008). Herons are strongly associated with magic, enchantment, hidden truths, divine messages, and mystery; they are especially associated with Manannan and the Cailleach (Anderson, 2008).

Blackbird (Irish – Lon Dubh)

Blackbirds are associated with Druids and witches, and were believed to be able to pass freely between our world and the Otherworld (Anderson, 2008). Blackbirds could open the Otherworld to a person, or place a person in a trance by singing, as well as being said to carry messages between worlds (Anderson, 2008).

References:

O hÓgain, D., (1995). Irish Superstitions.
Anderson, G., (2008). Birds of Ireland: Facts, Folklore & History
Carmichael, A., (1900). Carmina Gadelica

Chapter 6

Community

In both Druidism and heathenry, community is emphasized as a very important aspect of religion. For some people this is impossible due to geographic or demographic isolation, but for many people community is a matter of reaching out. Sometimes this reaching out occurs online and other times it may be in real life, but in both cases it brings with it both blessings and challenges. For anyone new to the often turbulent waters of pagan community there can be many hidden difficulties; this chapter looks at some of the more common issues you will probably run across and things to be aware of to help make your community experience a good one.

Discernment

One of the things you run across all the time on pagan groups, and something that often comes up in discussions, is recommended reading lists. This topic is something of a double edged sword because on the one hand there certainly are authors who should be recommended and ones who should be avoided, and on the other it is almost impossible to discuss authors without some personal bias creeping in. I have yet to see the subject of reading lists come up without it resulting in a debate about this or that book or author, usually to the utter befuddlement of several newer people who just don't understand what the big deal is.

Inevitably someone will say that every book has value, if only to inspire the spirituality of the reader. This comment always irks me because on the surface it is true, but that surface truth glosses over some significant issues. For one thing people, especially when they are just starting out, tend to take everything they read as true and when that first bit of knowledge is inaccurate it can be very difficult to unlearn it. It's also painful and embarrassing to learn something and then find out it's fairly commonly known in other areas to be false, made-up, or modern – like anything that came out of The White Goddess, The Blank Rune, the theory of the golden age of matriarchy, the 'nine million' dead in the inquisition, etc. Do these things have value? Sure, in their own way and with an understanding of their real history, yes. But the problem comes in when people are fed the lie and believe it, because we, as a community, have enough false histories and made up antiquity without choosing to perpetuate them ourselves. And another problem with the 'all books have value' theory is that some people never get beyond reading a handful of books, making the quality of those books very important. Let's face it if all you ever read is McCoy's Witta you are going to have some serious issues going forward. And quite frankly if you don't think it matters at all if a book has any accuracy or truth in it you may as well not bother reading any at all; just make it all up on your own and at least it will be genuinely your inspiration. Although I suppose that could bring up the problem of cults of personality that surround some authors – but that's probably a separate issue altogether.

So what is the solution? How do you decide what to read and whose recommendations to trust? The key is discernment. Everyone, beginner and long-time pagan or reconstructionist needs discernment to decide if a book or recommendation has value. Look at the book itself, the reviews it's gotten, talk to friends and ask around for opinions and take it all with a huge grain of salt; always use critical thinking skills. If you do get a book and read it question everything you read, especially if it's unfamiliar or seems 'off'. I regularly go to my friends and ask them their thoughts on tidbits from books – sometimes they agree with the information, sometimes they don't. It's sort of like the X-Files 'Trust No One' maxim, but over time you'll get a feel for what is solid information and what isn't and discernment is a vital thing to have. And this isn't just about historical information and accuracy; it's just as important for magical or ritual practice not to simply trust everything you read – or experience.

So we have discernment when it comes to written sources – which basically means how much you're going to believe someone else's opinion and how much trust you're going to put into the facts and theories they are putting forth. Critical thinking and common sense will be your best allies here, but what about discernment in other areas?

It always surprises me how people who are otherwise smart and cynical will believe, absolutely, any messages they get that comes from outside a human source, even if the message is being given through a human being. There seems to be some subconscious part of us that is afraid to question Gods or spirits, or even in some cases human 'experts' in spiritual or psychic matters. Obviously there is the aspect of this where people are merely being taken advantage of, such as the psychics who tell clients that they are cursed or being followed by an evil spirit and can only be 'helped' for a three-digit fee, but there are also situations where genuine spiritual contact is involved.

Spirits lie, with words and by omission, and messages coming through human beings are filtered through that person in a way that shapes the message. If you wouldn't trust a stranger who grabs you walking down the street and starts telling you to do things, why would you trust a spirit, or spiritual message? That isn't to say never trust such things, but don't just immediately assume if it's spiritual and from spirit it must be good. I have on a few occasions received messages from other spirit workers that were sound in the sense of the message, but that I could not safely do – for example I was told once to do ordeal work for Odin. That makes total sense given who and what he is, but because I have past issues with cutting, it is not safe for me to do the specific things I was told to do. Use common sense if you are ever told to do anything dangerous or that you feel unsafe about – just because it's coming from a spirit or deity doesn't mean it's written in stone. Don't be afraid to negotiate when you need to; you can offer something else, ask for help, look further into why, ask for alternatives... but don't just sit there and agree to things you don't want to do because you feel that once you've been told you have an obligation. You only have an obligation when you've made an oath, and even then paying a shild is an option if the oath absolutely cannot be kept.

I also don't understand why people hand over their free will when spirituality is involved (unless of course your path doesn't believe in it – not every one does). Personally I believe that we always have a choice in how we respond to messages, whether it's what we should learn about or do with our lives or a deity wanting our dedication. In mythology we can see multiple examples that this is so – Odin offers his aid and advice to King Hrolf Kraki who accepts it several times and then chooses to reject it, the Goddess of sovereignty comes to three brothers as a crone and the first two reject her but the third accepts her, the Queen of Faery offers Thomas the Rhymer a chance to go with her... of course choosing to accept or reject these offers each has its consequence. Both the cultures I seek to reconstruct, the Irish and the Norse, have ideas that relate to fate or destiny – more appropriately wyrd and dán – but not the set-in-stone Greek kind. Rather wyrd and dán, as I understand the concepts, are influenced by the choices we make. We shape our own fate through our actions or inactions, and this is as true of spirituality and spiritual dealings as anything else.

So, what to do? Personally I go to my friends for feedback, opinions, and confirmation – asking those who read cards or are intuitive to see what they get. When I am 'told' I need to do something I rarely trust a single source, but look for confirmation to validate that the message was accurate. Sometimes it turns out it was just me, my own projection or filter affecting things – or basically I saw what I wanted to see. Sometimes it is what it is and I can get more information or details from others. Community is an invaluable resource for things like this and over time you will start to build your own inner sense of discernment to get a feel for when to trust something and when to question it.

I hadn't intended to say anymore on this but recent discussions made me realize I left out one major area where discernment is vital and very underused... so let's start with a story...

I had made an appointment for an Ogham reading at a local pagan shop because, well, I had never run across an Ogham reader before and I couldn't resist. When I arrived for the appointment I was told the original reader was out sick but that another man was in also read Ogham so I agreed to see him instead. We went back and sat down and he began the normal introductory speech about what the Ogham are; as soon as politely possible I broke in and said I already knew what they were.

Reader: 'Oh, are you interested in Celtic things?'

Me: 'You could say that.'

Reader: 'If you ever want to really learn about Celtic magic or practice I'd be willing to take you on as a student. I'm the arch-Druid of the north-east and I mentor for the Ancient Order of Druids in America.'

Me: Blink. Blink.

This was the point when I should have used some discernment and politely gotten the heck out of there with my money, but sadly I chose to stay... and ended up reading for myself, after the 'reader' pulled out the book that came with the Ogham set and asked my opinion on the interpretation... but as soon as I left I emailed the AODA to confirm that he was telling the truth, or more to the point that he wasn't, about his claim of being a mentor for them. I received a very nice email back from John Michael Greer confirming my suspicion that his organization did not include this person as a member and that the man in no way taught or mentored for them.

The point of this story? Discernment extends to claims people make about themselves; we can't just blindly trust that people are what they say they are, and more importantly there is absolutely nothing wrong with checking on people's claims. I have several 'titles' which I don't often use but if I were to use them they could all be easily confirmed with the groups I belong to. For example, if I were to tell someone, perhaps at the next Pagan Pride Day, that I was a Druid that can be confirmed through my Order (the Order of the White Oak – you can check too). When someone claims to belong to a group or organization it can be checked; when they claim a specific title or position within a group that can also be checked. Don't be afraid to check. It isn't rude, especially if you are thinking of this person as a potential teacher.

So, you're asking, what about the things that can't be checked? If someone claims to be a solitary priestess or a Druid without a group affiliation? That is when discernment through observation comes in. Do they embody what they are claiming to be? If they do, good. If they don't then they aren't. Pretty much anyone can claim to be anything – claiming it doesn't make it true. Being it makes it true. This doesn't mean you have to do anything about your conclusion, necessarily, but if someone is claiming to deserve respect because of a false title you aren't obligated to give them special treatment or to excuse bad behavior. If someone is offering to teach you or include you in their group but they can't seem to find their butt with both hands you have every right to back away slowly and politely decline. And never surrender your own opinion to anyone just because they claim a big fancy title. It can be easy to get over-awed by a person throwing around impressive sounding credentials.

In the pagan community there seems to be this unspoken rule that we just take people at their word, but if the credentials are sound they will hold up to scrutiny, and if the person is what they say they are then you should know it because they should embody it.

Oh, and that whole 'archdruid of the north-east' thing? Some groups like ADF do have archdruids, but if someone claims to be the head of an entire pagan population without having a group affiliation it's pretty obviously BS. Anyone can claim to be the archdruid of the north-east, or the witch queen of Connecticut, or whatever... sounds impressive but it's nothing but ego talking.

Community Conundrums

How do we define who belongs to our community? Is it as simple as who we like and want to see as our community? Is it anyone who follows the same spirituality we do? Is it the larger pagan community? Or is it more subtle and complex than this? I don't actually have an answer yet, except that community is a nebulous thing that can include people where I live, people I choose to interact with, people online in groups I choose to belong to, and people with common interests to mine. Doesn't really clarify much, I know, but it's a work in progress.

I started wondering about this a little while back after someone began trolling a facebook group I was part of. Another person asked the troll to keep frith (peace) on the board and was promptly told that no frith was required on an imaginary group that didn't qualify for any rules of hospitality. Without digressing into a discussion of frith versus grith (sanctuary) in situations like that, I thought the situation raised some interesting questions about how we define community and how behave based on our definitions. Both CR and heathenry view hospitality – both being a good host and a good guest – as an important quality, as do many other cultures. Does this only apply when we feel like it does? Can we pick and choose the circumstances in which we must be polite, as the facebook troll said? Is it okay to be an obnoxious jerk outside our perceived community because hospitality somehow doesn't apply?

Personally I don't think so. I think that in the world we live in today nothing is as cut and dried as it *may have been* a thousand or two thousand years ago and our community is a fluid, shifting thing. I have people in my community who hold antithetical religious views, political views, and social views, but I still consider them a part of my community and I feel I owe them hospitality. I can't use my own religious views as an excuse to act like a jerk and then brush it off with, 'Oh, well, you aren't really part of my community so I don't owe you anything'.

Another key aspect of any reconstructionist community, CR or heathen, is a person's reputation and that is influenced by how someone treats other people inside and outside the community. Hospitality is one part of being an honorable person, in my opinion, and I don't think you can go into a situation with the attitude that it's okay to be dishonorable because the people you are dealing with aren't within your community. Maybe that is an odd sentiment for someone who is dedicated to Odin, but that's where I'm at with it right now. The Gods have a lot more leeway with some things than people do. Of course if someone else starts it first how you react to it is a different issue, but it's that initial approach, that first defining of what is appropriate based on who is and isn't part of the group that I'm thinking about. It's true that there is a structure to it, especially in heathenry with its clear ideas about innangard (inner community) and utgard (outsiders), but defining what falls where in a modern context can get very complicated... hence the conundrum...

The Dream of Pagan Unity and Why It's So Hard to Achieve

I've been thinking a lot lately about ecumenism among pagan groups; maybe it's the recent flurry of Pagan Pride Day planning, maybe it's the common refrain that so many people love to sing about wanting the community to all get along. Either way it's been on my mind a lot, because it seems that if everyone who wants unity among the various groups means what they say, then we would already have it; yet as a community we are divided in many different ways.

Some people are limited by their own views of those outside of their particular group or tradition, some are stuck in old feuds or in personality conflicts and some are simply stuck in the idea that their way is the only 'real' way. So how do we overcome this? It seems easy enough, if we could only get everyone to acknowledge their own hang-ups and issues with unity we could all pull together – but realistically can it be done? Should it be done? Are there compromises that simply should not be made, not even for so often dreamed of a goal as this one?

When I started writing this I began by thinking of my own biggest block, a particular local leader that I have a small laundry list of issues with. And I asked myself, can I let these go? Some of them, I can answer yes for even though it would take effort. I am capable of letting the past go if I really put some energy into it, especially when he never did me, personally, any direct harm. It wouldn't be easy but it could be done; however, if I am honest with myself there are other issues as well that I don't know if I could move past, ongoing things relating to integrity, truth in teaching – or I should say deception in teaching – and intentional perpetuation of ignorance that touch on areas where I have a much harder time looking the other way. And the bottom line of all this soul searching is that even when I try to put my personal feelings for this person aside, I am still left in a place where I do not want to be associated with him in any way.

How do we build community unity from that? And there is no other way; unity is not the same as tolerance. To be united as a community we must all stand together, and that is more than problematic when – in my own case – I have to always fight the urge to speak out against this person. How do we let go of the desire to let personal conflict and dislike interfere? How do we embrace community members that we simply do not like on a personal level?

How do we define our community? Who is in and who is out? Even within paganism, in the subgroups of traditions and religions, this is a massive issue. How do we define 'us'? We cannot hope to unite as a larger group of pagans until we figure out who we are as smaller individual groups and that seems an impossible task when every sub-group is fractured by inner disputes. Group self-definition is like the Holy Grail, everyone is searching for it but no one can really find it. Do we include or exclude people convicted of crimes? All crimes, or only some?

Do we push out the snake oil salesman and false prophets that are selling lies while proclaiming it the only 'real' witch-craft/heathenry/Druidism/etc., or would that very attempt put us on the same level of the more-pagan-than-thou types who cause so much dissention already? We must set boundaries for the safety of the community if nothing else, but how do we decide what those boundaries are and how do we enforce them?

As a group, pagans need to stop nitpicking each other; if another tradition has a different way of doing things that you disagree with on purely theological or personal grounds let it go. If it's not your group, why do you really care how they are doing things? If a group is engaging in dangerous, illegal, or manipulative practices that's a whole different issue, but differences in approach shouldn't matter. We waste way too much energy fighting over how other people do things, instead of looking for the common ground.

So I asked if pagan unity can be achieved, and I think the answer is yes, and no. Yes we can unite as a larger group if we find a way to put aside the differences that can be put aside, like letting go of the ideas that any one particular way is 'the' way, or the tradition. As soon as people start saying that they are the 'true' witches (Heathens/Druids/etc.) they have set up a rigid dichotomy of us against them and if you aren't with them then you aren't 'real' and therefore aren't legitimate, and that attitude has to go right from the start. I may not agree with someone, I may even hate everything about what they do and how they do it, but that doesn't make them less 'real'. Of course acknowledging that they are really pagan, or whatever they are identifying as, does not mean that anything they are saying is true or accurate. (There is also a deeper argument about people claiming to be part of initiatory traditions when they aren't – that isn't what I'm talking about here, I simply mean the broad labels like witch, or heathen or pagan that are largely matters of self-identification.) The flip side of that coin, and this is where the 'no' part of the answer comes in, is that some things can never be compromised and we as a community need to stop acting as if anyone calling themselves pagan is automatically a good person. People are people no matter what their faith and some pagans are good people and others are pretty crappy people, just like everyone else. It's okay for us to say, 'No, I won't be associated with that person,' if the reason is legitimate and we have really looked at whether we can compromise on this, but that means that true complete unity will never be possible because there will always be people identifying as pagans who contribute nothing but dissention to the community. There are online 'trolls' and there are real life ones, there are mentally unstable people, there are pedophiles and violent people, and there always will be and these are issues that the community will always have to contend with. Being pagan does not mean that all the bad in the world and in people just disappears, but we can acknowledge this fact and deal with it. So unity is a utopian idea, but building a strong ecumenical community isn't. That dream could be possible.

Building a larger community depends on putting aside the little things like personality conflict, pride, and mistrust of other traditions, and embracing the things we have in common. It means working together to build a larger sense of community, not to homogenize all the traditions into one; it's our diversity that makes us such an interesting group. Pagan community can be built and made strong, but not without real effort and soul searching from all of us – and that's why it remains a dream and not a reality.

Ní chaitheann an Chaint an T-éadach

Ní chaitheann an chaint an t-éadach.
The talk doesn't wear the clothes.
Traditional Irish proverb

I've talked a lot about community, what it is for pagans and reconstructionists, how we build it and define it. One thing I haven't talked about yet is how the individual fits into the community structure. I think there is often a perception of community as an entitlement; if you are pagan and a group is pagan then somehow acceptance should be immediate. This is not the reality and yet inevitably, when friction arises, individuals rarely seem to look at themselves and their own actions but point to the group as flawed. Maybe it's just me, because both CR and heathenry put a lot of emphasis on personal honor and responsibility, but when I have an issue with a community the first thing I do is review my own actions. What did I do that contributed to the situation? Could I have responded differently? Should I have? Sometimes I realize I was wrong in my actions or words and I apologize. Sometimes I realize that I would do it all the same. So it baffles me to see people enter a group, or stay in a group, who plow head on into a controversy – or create one – and then blame the group at large without ever acknowledging their own part. American culture is very individualized, so maybe it is that constant tension between wanting to fit into a group but also wanting to stand out as an individual. Maybe it is a lack of social skills by people who have been marginalized all their lives and expect the neopagan community to be a Utopian solution for all of their alienation.

Another aspect of this that I've been thinking about, especially in relation to online communities, is what inspired me to start with the quote that begins this section. The talk doesn't wear the clothes. It is so easy online to say things that are exaggerations at best and lies at worst. Sometimes it's simply people exaggerating their experience or activities, but other times it's the actual invention of events and titles that never existed. People talk a good game but in the end that talk always shows itself as empty, because there is no real substance to it. It's a dangerous game pretending to be who we aren't and sometimes that results in situations that cause fractures in the community. Of course there are also people whose talk doesn't reflect reality because they just aren't in touch with the reality the rest of us operate in. I mentioned this in my writing on discernment, but I personally never trust anyone who can't back up claims with outside sources; if you say you run a group I should be able to talk to other people in the group. If you say you wrote a book I should be able to find a copy of it. If you say you are the ordained grand high poobah of whatever there should be someone to confirm that. I'm Irish-American and I love a good brag, but without substance talk has no value. Without action words are just words. I actually have a lot more respect for the quiet ones who I know do a lot but don't talk much about it, because I know they do it. People who go around internet groups talking about cursing other people who disagree with them on the group, or challenging them to physical fights, amuse me to no end. Talk, talk, talk – no substance.

The talk doesn't wear the clothes – if we want to have anything worth talking about we have to actively live our spirituality. Our lives need to be a reflection of our values and our words should reflect our lives, not a fantasy of imagined deeds and actions. When we look at our words we should ask ourselves if they are a true representation of ourselves. Are we proud to have said them? Do we wish we hadn't?

Who wears your clothes – your actions or your talk?

Hospitality in a Modern World

Hospitality is an important quality in both Celtic and Norse traditions. In both cultures, as in many other ancient cultures, hospitality to guests was seen as an important social expectation. In the Norse Havamal we see a selection of advice given in how to live honorably, including this part about hospitality:

134. I counsel thee, Stray-Singer, accept my counsels,
they will be thy boon if thou obey'st them,
they will work thy weal if thou win'st them:
growl not at guests, nor drive them from the gate
but show thyself gentle to the poor.
135. Mighty is the bar to be moved away
for the entering in of all.
Shower thy wealth, or men shall wish thee
every ill in thy limbs.
(Bellows translation)

In the Cath Maige Tuired it is a lack of hospitality that is at the root of the second battle between the Fomorians and the Tuatha Dé Danann, as the lack of hospitality by the half-Fomorian King Bres eventually resulted in a rebellion by the Tuatha Dé Danann.

36. At that time, Bres held the sovereignty as it had been granted to him. There was great murmuring against him among his maternal kinsmen the Tuatha Dé Danann, for their knives were not greased by him. However frequently they might come, their breaths did not smell of ale; and they did not see their poets nor their bards nor their satirists nor their harpers nor their pipers nor their horn-blowers nor their jugglers nor their fools entertaining them in the household. They did not go to contests of those pre-eminent in the arts, nor did they see their warriors proving their skill at arms before the king, except for one man, Ogma the son of Lain.

39. On one occasion the poet came to the house of Bres seeking hospitality (that is, Coirpre son of Etain, the poet of the Tuatha De). He entered a narrow, black, dark little house; and there was neither fire nor furniture nor bedding in it. Three small cakes were brought to him on a little dish–and they were dry. The next day he arose, and he was not thankful. As he went across the yard he said,

'Without food quickly on a dish,
Without cow's milk on which a calf grows,
Without a man's habitation after darkness remains,
Without paying a company of storytellers – let that be Bres's condition.'

(Gray's translation)

These are just a few examples of the way that the value of hospitality was expressed in common stories in both cultures. In the first example we see the idea that how we act as a host to our guests reflects on our reputation for good or ill. In the second we see the consequences of failing to offer hospitality when it is expected. In both cases we can see that hospitality involves generosity and openness to guests and that failing to be hospitable opens a person up to consequences of both reputation and (in the Irish) satire. It's clear from this and from other material relating to hospitality in these groups that hospitality was important and most modern pagans and reconstructionists seem to agree with the value of this. Yet how do we, as modern followers of these older ways, create hospitality in our lives? How do we embrace a virtue of open handed giving and welcome to guests in a culture (talking about America in particular) that is often not reflective of that same value?

The weekend before I wrote this, my oldest daughter, who is eight, had a friend over for a play date. I spent a lot of the visit reminding my daughter that her guest *was* a guest, and was to be treated as such. When there was only one cookie left, it went to her friend. When they could not agree on a game to play I intervened and said that as the guest her friend should be allowed to choose what to do. This is how I was raised and I feel it is in line with the older values of hospitality, so it is what I want to pass on to my children; however, I found out after the other child had left that this is not the usual way of things in modern society. My daughter informed me that when she went to other children's homes she had to do whatever they wanted to do, and was basically treated by the parents as imported entertainment for the other child. I was not happy to find this out, although it gave me an opportunity to discuss the value of being a good guest as well. Of course I also wasn't happy to find out that this child, much like another of my daughter's friends that had come over previously, attempted to steal something while she was here. The whole situation has me thinking about the subject of hospitality and how we, as modern pagans, can create a culture of hospitality – particularly for our children – in a world that is often at odds with those values.

So far my best solution is to read the stories that I can to my children that emphasize these values and to try to show them by example what hospitality means to me. And what I would like it to mean to them. It's a complex subject, since hospitality is a balance between being a good host and a good guest, and to violate either has consequences, so conveying this to a child growing up in what amounts to a different culture with different values is challenging.

How do you find that balance in your own life? How much value do you place on hospitality and being a good guest? And how can we, as modern pagans, re-establish this value within our own community? Just some food for thought...

References:

Bellows translation of the Havamal can be found at http://www.pitt.edu/~dash/havamal.html

Gray's translation of the Cath Maige tuired can be found at http://www.sacred-texts.com/neu/cmt/cmteng.htm

Contemplations on 'Enough'

You know whatever path we walk in life, whatever spirituality we follow there always seems to be someone – or a couple of people even – telling us it's not the right path for us. Usually the argument boils down to being told you aren't enough of something; you don't have enough ancestry, you don't have enough of a connection, enough of an understanding, enough experience, enough approval. Not enough, kid, sorry go look somewhere else, or call it something else... and in that moment it always hits hard, that feeling of being judged and found unworthy.

The thing is we are all faced with these challenges, we are all judged as not 'enough' by someone somewhere. And when we face that challenge there are two ways to respond; you can let the other person's judgment control you or you can look deep inside and decide for yourself. It easy enough to fold under the pressure and say that the other person must be right, to see ourselves as less because someone else is telling us we are. That's the easy way, for sure. But the better way, I think, is to look inside and see for yourself what you find there. The temple of Apollo at Delphi had the words 'gnothi seauton' carved above the entrance, 'know thyself', and it's a good aphorism to live by. Know yourself, and judge for yourself whether you are enough... and if you find yourself not enough than do some soul searching about why that is and what you can do about it. Some of the most profound insights I have had about who I am and what my spirituality is have come from being judged not enough by others, because it is through that challenge that I am forced to really look at myself and what I am doing and decide *for myself* whether I am enough or not. Sometimes I found that the other person was right, that my own path had taken me away from what I was identifying as and into something new and different, or even that I had misunderstood the entire thing from the beginning. Sometimes these moments can offer an opportunity to re-assess and find firmer footing or a new approach, even help to find a whole new direction to go in or re-connect to roots we had lost over time. Other times I found that I was indeed exactly where I needed to be and that being challenged on it actually made my connection stronger by drawing my attention to it. Finding the Truth in these moments is a matter of honest reflection, of letting go of what I want and seeing what is actually there.

Being enough or not enough is a choice we make, because in the end the only person who can really make us unworthy is ourselves.

Chapter 7

Miscellaneous Thoughts

Mistletoe and the Druids

One of the most well known plants associated with the Druids is mistletoe (Viscum Album), yet what do we really know about this plant and its connection to the Celts and their priests?

Well, the main source of our knowledge connecting the two is Pliny the Elder who writes about it in his Natural History. For the sake of completeness I am going to include everything Pliny said about mistletoe here:

> *Upon this occasion we must not omit to mention the admiration that is lavished upon this plant by the Gauls. The Druids – for that is the name they give to their magicians – held nothing more sacred than the mistletoe and the tree that bears it, supposing always that tree to be the robur [oak]. Of itself the robur is selected by them to form whole groves, and they perform none of their religious rites without employing branches of it; so much so, that it is very probable that the priests themselves may have received their name from the Greek name for that tree. In fact, it is the notion with them that everything that grows on it has been sent immediately from heaven, and that the mistletoe upon it is a proof that the tree has been selected by God himself as an object of his especial favor.*
>
> *The mistletoe, however, is but rarely found upon the robur; and when found, is gathered with rites replete with religious awe. This is done more particularly on the fifth day of the moon, the day which is the beginning of their months and years, as also of their ages, which, with them, are but thirty years. This day they select because the moon, though not yet in the middle of her course, has already considerable power and influence; and they call her by a name which signifies, in their language, the all-healing. Having made all due*

preparation for the sacrifice and a banquet beneath the trees, they bring thither two white bulls, the horns of which are bound then for the first time. Clad in a white robe the priest ascends the tree, and cuts the mistletoe with a golden sickle, which is received by others in a white cloak. They then immolate the victims, offering up their prayers that God will render this gift of his propitious to those to whom he has so granted it. It is the belief with them that the mistletoe, taken in drink, will impart fecundity to all animals that are barren, and that it is an antidote for all poisons. Such are the religious feelings which we find entertained towards trifling objects among nearly all nations.

So from this we can learn that the Gaulish Druids who Pliny was writing about considered the oak sacred and the mistletoe which grew upon it to be divinely given, possibly because of its rarity. Whenever mistletoe was found on oaks it would then be gathered with due ceremony on the next appropriate day, which appears to be just before the first quarter of the moon, when, as Pliny says, the moon has power and influence. To me this is another interesting celestial connection with the mistletoe. The plant would then be gathered with great ceremony, including a feast and the sacrifice of two bulls. Pliny also mentions the use of a golden sickle. However, gold is far too soft to be used in a cutting tool – many people assume then that the sickle must have been of iron, but since there were also prohibitions in later Celtic folklore about cutting herbs with cold iron I rather think it is more likely that the sickle was bronze, perhaps inlaid or coated with gold. (Incidentally Pliny notes, as does Caesar in his Gallic Wars, that the Celts measured time by nights instead of days and began months and years also in such a way.)

Mistletoe itself is a parasitic plant that grows in trees, rooting from seeds usually spread by birds. It grows to form a mass of twigs and leaves about two to three feet wide, flowers in May and produces berries between late November and December, which are a waxy white in color. There is some debate about when the Druids may have collected mistletoe, as some folkloric accounts mention it being gathered around New Year's Day (although whether this means Samhain or January 1st is unclear) although it would seem logical that the easiest time to gather it would have been in the fall or winter. As the book The Trees of Old England says, 'In summer we seldom notice that mistletoe is living within the foliage of the tree it inhabits, not until autumn has stripped all away, and winter has rendered the woods transparent... do we discover its presence.' Our only firm account of Druids harvesting mistletoe is Pliny and he makes no mention at all of the time of year or season, but does say that it was gathered whenever it was found, leading me to believe that there was no specific seasonal rite relating to it. I think it is possible that the later idea of the Druids collecting mistletoe at the start of the New Year may have been a confusion of Pliny including a reference to the Celtic days, months and years beginning with the new moon with his discussion of the mistletoe being collected.

Folklore associates mistletoe with protection from all evil influences and it is also a symbol of fertility, something that is mentioned in Pliny's account, and may lend itself to the folk belief of kissing under the mistletoe. Additionally the stem and leaves had a wide variety of medicinal uses that can be documented back at least 500 years, and in folklore and practice longer. Culpepper's herbal from the 1600s mentions, 'Tragus saith, that the fresh wood of many mistletoe bruised, and the juice drawn forth and dropped in the ears that hath imposthumes in them doth help to ease them within a few days.' According to Grieve's Modern Herbal, mistletoe has been written about as a folk remedy in France and Britain since at least 1682. The stem and leaves – collected before the berries form – were used and it was believed to treat epilepsy and calm nervous disorders and treat heart conditions. It is noted that the berries have the opposite effect and are not recommended for use, although external use of the berries as a paste is mentioned. The berries are toxic and produce extreme intestinal discomfort, seizures, delirium, and heart problems in high doses.

The true connection between the Druids and mistletoe may always be something of a mystery, but it does seem that it played a role in Gaulish and possibly British belief and practice (not existing in Ireland). Examining the evidence we do have, thin as it may be, is none the less interesting and enlightening and shows us the possible reverence of a plant that was born of the sky and blessed by the Gods, connected to a sacred tree, and with known healing applications.

References:

Culpepper's Herbal (1649) reprinted 1983
Grieve, M., (1931). A Modern Herbal
http://www.maryjones.us/ctexts/classical_pliny.html
http://www.dalswildlifesite.com/themistletoe.htm

The Use of Stones and Crystals in Celtic Tradition

In modern neopaganism and the new age movement, using crystals and stones for healing is an almost ubiquitous practice. This can lead people who focus more on reconstruction to wonder what place this practice held, if any, with the ancients, in my case specifically the Irish and closely related Celtic cultures. When we look at the oldest sources, the accounts of the Greek and Roman writers, all that is found is a reference to the fabled 'Druid's Egg',[12] an object that may or may not actually be a stone, said to be formed by the spit of snakes. On the other hand when we look at slightly more recent folk practices from Ireland and Scotland we can find evidence of the use of stones and crystals for several purposes.

Archeologists excavating Iron Age graves in England have found balls of 'rock crystal' (clear quartz, I think) wrapped in bands of silver, or less often gold or bronze (Fraser Black, 1894). It is unknown what these were used for, whether they held a magical significance or were purely decorative; however, similar balls of crystal were used in later periods in the belief that they could ensure victory in battle or bring healing. In Glenlyon there was such a wrapped crystal that was called either 'Clach Bhaui' (powerful stone) or 'Clach Buaidh' (victory stone); similarly another such stone is called the 'Clach-na-Bratach' (stone of the standard) (Fraser Black, 1894). The Clach-na-Bratach belongs to Clan Donnachaidh; it was found by the clan chief in 1315 on the way to battle and was believed to be a good omen, as such it was consulted before every following battle and carried into the fray until 1715 when an internal flaw was noted (Fraser Black, 1894). After it was retired from battle it was believed that this stone also had healing powers, especially for cattle. There is also a named stone in Scotland called the Clach Dearg (red stone) which is reputed to have the ability to charge water with healing power, following a certain ritual process (Fraser Black, 1894). Some say the Clach Dearg was originally part of the wand of an arch Druid, while others believe it was imported from the east (McNeill, 1956). In Keppoch the MacKenzies are said to possess a healing stone associated with the holy well of Brighid, which would be dipped into the water from the well for a healing charm (McNeill, 1956). The majority of these stones range in size from one inch across to an inch and a half, and most are mounted with silver bands.

When used for healing purposes we see both the above described crystals and also references to similarly sized but more oval or egg shaped crystals being used. Cure stones might be used in one of two ways, either dipped in water which was then drunk or otherwise used on the afflicted person or animal, or rubbed directly on the injured or ill body part. When used in water the stone was often wrapped with silver bands, usually four, with a loop for hanging or wearing; the crystal would be dipped into water, while the person chanted:

Let me dip thee in the water
Thou yellow, beautiful gem of power!
In water of purest wave,
Which Bridget didn't permit to be contaminated.
In the name of the Apostles twelve,
In the name of Mary, Virgin of virtues,
And in the name of the High Trinity
And all the shining angels,
A blessing on the gem,
A blessing in the water, and
A healing of bodily ailments to each suffering creature.
(Fraser Black, 1894)

For my own purposes I prefer to use a slightly different version:

Let me dip you in the water
You beautiful gem of power!
In water of purest wave,
Which Brighid kept pure.
A blessing on the gem,
A blessing in the water, and
A healing of bodily ailments
to each suffering creature.

Besides these crystals there is also a history of the use of other types of stones for healing. Generally the type of stone didn't matter, as they appear to be simple river stones or pebbles, but often the color seemed to be significant, with white as the most common, and black, green, and red also described. While color is the most common descriptive point there are specific examples in Scottish Charms and Amulets of certain types of stone used for certain purposes:

'Iron stone' (possibly hematite or iron ore?): cure all, held
Basalt: healing horses
Jet: curing diseases
Shale/coal: holed, protecting animals from witchcraft
Fossilized shells: arthritis
Flint: general ailments
Amber: general healing, cure for snake bites, used for people and animals
Quartz: heal all, victory, cures infertility

Both Saints Columba and Fillan were said to possess 'curing stones', all white, which could heal when dipped in water that was then consumed. Saint Molio also possessed such a healing stone, but that one was green and was rubbed on the afflicted area to effect a cure; interestingly this stone is also said to grant victory in battle and is alleged to have belonged to Clan McDonald. Many churches had healing stones on their altars, and some could be found next to holy wells; these might resemble the body part they were best used to heal, such as the eye or heart (McNeill, 1956).

In Scotland there are also accounts of several named curing stones: Clach Leigh (medicine stone) was a green tinged stone, Clach Ruaidhe (red stone) was used for healing cows by rubbing it on the udder, and the Clach Spotaiche (spotted stone) was a piece of black basalt that was used in healing horses (Fraser Black, 1894). Whenever these or similar healing stones were used by rubbing a charm might be said at the same time, such as this one from Strathspey:

Gu maith an diugh, 's fhearr am maireach;
An deigh sin gun dad ach 'n larach.
(This day well, next better,
After that nothing but a scar)
(Fraser Black, 1894)

A similar use can be seen in Irish lore, but instead of a known curing stone, all the person needs is to find three green stones in a running stream, after midnight but before dawn, and in silence. These stones are rubbed on the afflicted body part, from the top down towards the feet, while the person chants:

Wear away, wear away,
There you shall not stay,
Cruel pain – away, away
(Wilde, 1896)

Less commonly curing stones might be used for other purposes. A type of curing stone was one used for curing infertility. One example from Scotland is an egg shaped quartz that was passed from one 'wise woman' to another upon death, and was used by placing the stone in running water (preferably south-flowing) in which the woman would then wash her feet (Fraser Black, 1894). Stones of rock crystal would also be drilled to create a hole and then worn to protect against the evil eye (McNeill, 1956). The famed stone of the Brahan Seer was a white stone with a hole in it, said to be a gift of the fairies, through which he could divine the future (McNeill, 1956).

These stones are described as being worn and carried in the pocket, but may also receive special care. One curing stone was said to be kept in a locked chest, wrapped in linen and then wool (Fraser Black, 1894). Another was said to be wrapped in cloth, kept in a silk bag, and wrapped in a napkin (Fraser Black, 1894). In many cases they were passed down in families as an heirloom, and if they were well known people might come from great distances away for the offered healing.

References:

Fraser Black, G., (1894). Scottish Charms and Amulets
McNeill, F., (1956). The Silver Bough, volume 1

Wilde, (1991). Irish Cures, Mystic Charms & Superstitions

Saint Patrick's Day, Snakes, and Irish-American Pride

For the last several years there has been a large controversy about Saint Patrick's Day within the pagan community. In 2012 there were anti-Saint Pat's day events and such on facebook created by people, very sincere people, who believe Saint Patrick to be some sort of super powered anti-pagan figure who drove out the Druids of Ireland and broke the back of paganism there. The general consensus by the people who share that thought seems to be that March 17th every year should be a day of black-clad mourning for Irish paganism or a day of protest against... well, against something. Now I have absolutely no issue with the way anyone wants to spend their March 17th, I generally favor wearing black, and I certainly agree that by and large Saint Pat's day in America is a hideous neon green tourist event. However, I am something of a stickler for history – as some of you may have noticed by now – and I don't like seeing false history becoming mainstream, nor do I like my own actions on March 17th being judged as wrong because of someone else's views, as I have been told previously that my celebrating the day is offensive and disrespectful. So the past few years I have tried, in comments here and there, to point out the history and the Truth to give people a better understanding of how things really happened so that they can move forward and decide what to do with some solid information instead of emotion. For the purpose of this article I am just going to lay the facts out and explain my own position and let everyone judge for themselves. I am not trying to change anyone's opinion or start a fight – I am only offering the history of who Saint Patrick really was, what he really did, how he interacted with the Druids, and what the bit about the snakes was about. I'm also going to talk a little about why and how I celebrate March 17, and what it means to me.

So let's begin with a little history. Back somewhere around the end of the 4th century in Britain – no one knows exactly where, except that it was likely on the coast – a boy named Maewyn Succat was born to a wealthy Roman official named Calpurius (Awesome Stories, 2012). Maewyn was born into a Christian family but he didn't consider himself especially devout. When he was 16 he was kidnapped, along with many other people from his father's household, and taken into slavery in Ireland where he was made a shepherd (Saint Patrick, nd). Among the hills and sheep Maewyn found solace in his father's religion, before eventually escaping after six years and making his way, eventually, back to Britain where he joined the church (Awesome Stories, 2012). At some point Maewyn took the name Particius, later anglicized to Patrick, and decided that he had a calling from his God to return to Ireland to preach to the people there (Awesome Stories, 2012). Unlike the common belief though, Patrick wasn't the first Bishop in Ireland – there were several previous bishops including Pallidius who was sent by the Pope in 429 (O hÓgain, 1999). At this point in the early 5th century Ireland already had a small but settled Christian population complete with churches, monasteries, priests and bishops (O hÓgain, 1999). In any event Patrick returned to Ireland and traveled around trying to establish himself. He claims to have had some success and baptized 'thousands' of people – of course he also had many difficulties including, apparently, being accused of accepting money for baptisms and other bribes as well as being beaten and robbed and repeatedly threatened with death (Saint Patrick, nd). Unlike the other Irish Christians of the time Patrick was an evangelist and did seek to convert people, but in his 30 years of ministry in Ireland he did not seem to have had any stunning success; probably because the Irish did not seem overly concerned with or threatened by Christianity and may have initially just incorporated it along with their pagan beliefs (Da Silva, 2009). After Patrick's death, most likely on March 17th 461, very little was written about him for several hundred years.

Ireland remained pagan for another eight or nine generations before the population became mostly Christian – and that was when the tale of Patrick really took off. In the 7th century, about 200 years after Patrick died, his hagiography was written, The Life of Saint Patrick by Muirchu maccu Mactheni, and the Patrick of Muirchu's story was very different than the historical Patrick, so much so that modern scholars now differentiate between the two (Da Silva, 2009). Muirchu's Patrick was a bold, vindictive, confrontational wonder-worker who performed miracles and was said to have destroyed the Druids in Ireland (O hÓgain, 1999). This mythic Patrick – unlike the humble historical Patrick who authored the Confessio – lost no opportunity to curse those who defied him or kill those who opposed him. In one of the stories in The Life of Saint Patrick, for example, the saint uses his God's 'power' to crush a Druid's skull and calls an earthquake to kill many others (Da Silva, 2009). In another tale Patrick was said to have turned himself and his entire retinue into deer to escape pursuit. It should be pretty obvious that this is pure invention, something to appeal to a 7th century audience looking to hear about wonders and drama on par with the other Irish myths, but not anything relating to actual events. In fact some scholars have pointed out that had Patrick actually gone in and tried to convert by the sword he would have ended up martyred for his trouble. To quote the excellent article by Da Silva:

> *It is clear that the pagan Irish would not have tolerated the behavior of the mythical Saint Patrick. There was no way Patrick could use coercion or the threat of force as part of his strategy to convert the pagans. E. A. Thompson writes that 'the pagans were far too powerful and menacing... And he was doubtlessly aware that if he gave any sign of trying to impose his views on the Irish pagans against their will, his mission would come to an abrupt and bloody end' (90).*
>
> (Da Silva, 2009)

The point to all of this is that the Patrick we are familiar with today is mostly a mythic figure, created by a great PR department. The historical Patrick didn't actually do very much and it wasn't until hundreds of years later, when politics in some of the churches he founded meant the need for a powerful figure, and the Church was looking to complete the conversion of the remaining pagans, that he was reinvented as the super-saint we know today. Many aspects of Saint Patrick's story seem as well to involve the saint being inserted into older mythology, such as in some of the stories surrounding Lughnasa where saint Patrick takes over the role of Lugh in fighting off the forces of darkness and chaos to secure the harvest (MacNeill, 1962). This would have been a logical substitution over time as the new religion replaced the old. Beyond that I have my own idea about how a British born Roman ended up as the patron saint of Ireland, but that probably falls into the realm of a conspiracy theory so I'll leave it off.

Why does all this matter to me? Well, for one I have always felt strongly that bad history does paganism no favors. For another thing I can't see any purpose to feeling outraged today over something that didn't even actually happen 1,560 years ago, or for that matter demonizing someone who didn't actually do very much. I just don't see any point in buying into another faith's mythology in a way that creates feelings of anger and negativity in my own. I am an Irish pagan and I am a Druid and I know from studying history that both Irish paganism and Druidism went on well after Patrick, that his life as we know it today is just a fancy story made up to replace older myths, and that in the end Patrick has no more meaning to me than what I give him. Why should I give him power over my life by believing he was greater than he was? I admire his devotion to his own faith and his courage in going back to a country where he had been taken by force as a slave, but beyond that he's just another historical figure in a sea of historical figures.

Now on to the snakes. Another big aspect of Saint Patrick's Day for pagans is the idea that the story of Patrick driving the snakes out of Ireland was actually an allegory for his driving out of the Druids. This idea is pretty well integrated into media and common belief; many people repeat it and there are even modern celebrations of 'All Snakes Day' in honor of the triumphant return of the modern Druids. Now, I am all in favor of the snake as a modern symbol of Druids – plenty of wonderful symbolism there since snakes are energized by the sun and 'reborn' each spring out of the earth after hibernating, eat little fluffy things, often are passed by unseen, not to mention the more obvious associations with wisdom and the historic Gaulish Druid's eggs – and I think the idea of a modern All Snakes Day is pretty cool. The history, though, just isn't there for any connection either of Saint Patrick with snakes or of the story being about Druids. Firstly, Ireland hasn't had snakes since before the last ice age, so there never were any snakes to be driven out by anyone, immediately indicating that this is likely another magical addition to his story (National Zoo, n.d.). Second of all, and more importantly, the actual story from Patrick's hagiography says that he drove out the snakes and toads (toads being very rare and snakes as we've established being non-existent) (Banruadh, 2006). For people living in Ireland after Patrick this story would have been a great explanation of why those animals weren't in Ireland, because there is no reason to think the 7th century story was an allegory. Quite frankly the rest of Patrick's hagiography has him dueling Druids right and left, killing those who oppose him with callous righteousness, so why would the story suddenly get cryptic about him driving the Druids out? Every other page was proclaiming it proudly! No, this particular tidbit – which is suspiciously exactly the same as a story from the life of a French saint – was always meant to be literal. The earliest reference I have found to anyone thinking the snakes meant Druids (and thanks to the friend who helped me find it) is in The Fairy Faith in Celtic Countries from 1911 where someone states that he believes, based on a story, that because a certain place was the location of the Druids' last stronghold and was also the place from which Saint Patrick drove out snakes, that the snakes must represent the Druids, but it's just faulty logic (Evans Wentz, 1911). The snakes in the story were just meant to be snakes, just as the toads were toads and Saint George's dragon was a dragon.

So why do I celebrate Saint Patrick's day? That's a good question, since I am certainly no Catholic. But the truth is that I have celebrated a secular version of St. Pat's day for my entire life; in my family it was a celebration of our Irish heritage, a day when we told stories about the family, ate traditional Irish-American food and enjoyed each other's company. I have been pagan since I was 11, but I never questioned the validity of celebrating my heritage with my family. Sure my heritage is what it is every day of the year, but that was one special day when the whole family celebrated together. My father and I would go out and enjoy a show together, the Wolfetones one year, the Irish Tenors several times, a wide array of different Irish step dancing groups. When I was young we would go out to dinner for corned beef and cabbage and after my grandmother came to this area we would go to her house and she would cook for everyone. I have so many wonderful, happy memories of all the Saint Patrick's days I've had with the people I love and that is why I celebrate it, and why I will continue to – because it's a family tradition. One I hope to pass on to my own children. We're Irish-Americans every day of the year, but March 17th is the one day when we are most aware of it, of our roots, of our history. Of our traditions.

The year that I am writing this, my family, my husband and daughters and I, will be going to eat corned beef and cabbage at my grandmother's house. She is 94 now, but she still cooks on St. Pat's day all the same. We'll tell stories about the family and about past celebrations, and when we get home my daughters and I will light candles on our ancestor altar in honor of the family that isn't with us physically any more. And on the 18th I will go with my oldest daughter to see Celtic Woman in concert (the first time since my dad died I've gone to a show for Saint Patrick's day, but that's a tradition that needs continuing).

Now in a modern setting we have All Snakes Day as a pagan alternative to St. Pat's day; I don't generally celebrate it only because it tends to emphasize the snakes-equals-Druids idea, although not everyone who celebrates it believes that, to be fair. Another alternative that is gaining popularity is to call it something like Irish Heritage Day because the emphasis of the day to Irish pagans is to celebrate that and that certainly captures the spirit of the holiday for most Americans. I rather like that one, and sometimes use it myself. Finally there has been a movement based in the old ideas about hero-cults to celebrate the 17th of March in honor of great Irish mythic heroes like Cu Chulain. I find that idea intriguing and intend to look into it more.

References:

http://www.awesomestories.com/religion/st-patrick-of-st-patricks-day/maewyn-succat—kidnapping-victim

Saint Patrick (n.d.) Saint Patrick's Confession http://www.cin.org/patrick.html

Da Silva, B., (2009). Saint Patrick, the Irish Druids, and Ireland Conversion to Christianity http://www.strangehorizons.com/2009/20090727/da_silva-a.shtml

Ó Hógáin, D., (1999). The Sacred Isle

MacNeill, M., (1962). The Festival of Lughnasa

Evans Wentz, W. Y., (1911). The Fairy Faith in Celtic Countries http://www.sacred-texts.com/neu/celt/ffcc/ffcc310.htm

http://branruadh.blogspot.com/2006/03/so-i-have-promised-so-i-have-done.html

http://nationalzoo.si.edu/Animals/ReptilesAmphibians/NewsEvents/irelandsnakes.cfm

Thoughts on The Ogham Tract

The Ogham Tract is one of the most interesting and useful texts to study for those interested in Irish mythology and divination. Within the text the mythological origins of Ogham are outlined and several different types of Ogham are discussed, although only the Tree Ogham and Word Oghams are gone into with any depth. The sections detailing these two types of Ogham are invaluable, however, for those who seek to use the Ogham for divination since they attach significant meaning to each letter, and these meanings can be used as the basis for a system of symbolism.

The first section looks at the mythological history of the Ogham, using the typical question and answer style so often seen in Irish texts. The first question asks about the place, time, inventor and cause of the creation of the Ogham and the answers, while apocryphal, are illuminating. We learn that the Ogham was created in Ireland during the time that Bres ruled the Tuatha Dé Danann, before mortals came to Ireland, and that it was invented by the God Ogma to prove his inventiveness and to give the educated something the uneducated didn't have. This tells us not only that the Ogham is believed to have divine origins, but also that it is believed to have been created as something to be reserved for a select few. The second questions asked relate to why it is called Ogham, who are the 'father' and 'mother' of the Ogham, what was first written in it and why 'b' is the primary letter. The name is explained as a play on words from og-uaim meaning perfect alliteration and is an allusion to the poet's art and possibly the very mnemonics that are used to remember the meanings of each letter in each type of Ogham. The father of Ogham is, of course, Ogma, and the mother is said to be his hand or blade; this is a beautiful description of the balanced act of creation involving both passive design and active carving. The final answer contains another fascinating bit of mythology, that is that the first thing written was 'b' and that it was written as a warning to the God Lugh that his wife was about to be kidnapped to Faery. Interestingly it is said that 'b', which in tree Ogham is associated with birch, was written seven times on a switch of birch; this not only reinforces the connection between the letter and the tree but also offers a possible magic charm to be used.

After this section the divisions of Ogham are discussed, with the idea of dividing the Ogham into four groups of five. It also mentioned that they can be separated into three groups of eight based on the Tree Ogham, divided by chieftain trees, peasant trees, and shrub trees. A second origin of Ogham is mentioned, the school of Fenius, which adds three dipthongs to the 20 consonants and vowels. Then a brief outline of the Tree Ogham is given, followed by the more in-depth description of the Tree and Word Oghams, and then very brief descriptions of many other types of Ogham.

By studying the trees associated with each letter and then the descriptions given for each correspondence to the Word Ogham, a clear pattern of symbols can be developed for use in divination. Using the Ogham for divination can be effective and useful if the symbolism of each letter is fully understood. Many people err in only looking to the Tree Ogham for meaning when divining with the letters, when in fact the other types of Ogham reinforce and add detail and depth of meaning providing clearer readings. Ogham can easily be used as the primary means of divination for both personal daily use and at ritual, but it is important to understand the meanings of each letter as fully as possible. Interestingly the 'Boy Ogham' is actually a method of divination in and of itself that uses the mother's name written in Ogham to predict the gender of her unborn child by dividing the name at a certain point, which is unfortunately not specified in the text.

The Ogham Tract may at first seem of interest only to those seeking to learn about divination since that is what Ogham is most known for these days, yet the tract contains valuable mythology as well. Studying this text is useful to anyone because it expands our knowledge of Irish mythology with small details and also highlights the exclusive place of Ogham literacy when the Tract was written. And, of course, it is invaluable for those seeking to use the Ogham for divination as well. No matter what your focus is, if you are interested in studying the Ogham, this text is useful and should be studied.

References:

Laurie, E., (2007). Ogam: Weaving Words of Wisdom
Montfort, P., (2002). Ogam: The Celtic Oracle of the Trees
Ellison, R., (2008). Ogham, the Secret Language of the Druids
Blamires, S.,(1997). Celtic Tree Mysteries, Secrets of the Ogham
Thorson, E., (1992). The Book of Ogham

Weeping for the Stone

I try to be philosophical about the vagaries of life. Bad things happen, and often these bad things are senseless, and there is just as often nothing constructive to be done. War and death and suffering are a constant of life and as much as I might detest them, as much as I might hate watching the news and seeing them, there is little to do but keep on going. Maybe it's a type of desensitization, a way to avoid constantly dwelling on things I can't change. Life goes on, and I try to keep that perspective. Sometimes, though, an event will occur that – for whatever reason – sticks with me, digs in, something that I just can't let go of.

As I write these words, I have just read that the Lia Fal on the hill of Tara in Ireland had been defaced, attacked with a hammer, causing damage to all four sides of the stone. Reading the article caused an immediate and visceral reaction, a blend of grief and anger that simply will not go away. It saddens me that the stone is permanently changed, damaged, although I appreciate that it could have been much worse. It makes me furious that this damage was intentional, an act of focused will by a person, who repeatedly bashed at the stone. I want justice for the spirit of that place, but more than that I want vengeance. I felt the same way a year and a half previously, when someone cut down the sacred thorn tree in Glastonbury. As I write this, they have not yet caught the people responsible for felling the thorn tree and I suspect they will never find out who hammered chunks out of the Lia Fal. It's appalling to me that anyone could do these things, and more than that I don't understand why. Why do people feel the need to destroy things that are significant to other people? What purpose does it serve to destroy an irreplaceable 3,500-year-old standing stone? Of course my head knows it could have been for anything from a political statement to drunken mischief, but my heart revolves over and over on the permanence of it. I don't agree with or advocate anyone destroying anyone else's sacred history – whether its ancient monuments to Buddha or historic churches – no matter what reason the perpetrators come up with.

Places have spirits, and sacred places have a special spirit to them, a feeling that is unique. Historic places that have seen people coming and worshipping or paying them honor for hundreds of years, or even millennia, have an energy that is an extension of this spirit, in my experience. I think that is why people are drawn to travel to sacred places, to touch the stone and wood that our ancestors have touched back through the ages. There is a feeling of connection that comes from experiencing a sacred site that grounds us, that makes our faith tangible. It is tragic to see that connection attacked, that sacred place desecrated, whether or not it is myth or fact that makes it sacred.

As an Irish (and Norse) pagan there are a few sacred places that I want to go to before I die, to feel that energy, to know the spirit of that place, and to connect to the pagan Gods in their old holy places. One day I will travel to Ireland, and I will walk up the hill at Tara and touch the Stone of Destiny, as legend says the old high kings did, as the stories say the Gods themselves did in bringing the stone to Ireland from Falias. This is something I have dreamed of doing for many years but have never yet done. I felt increased urgency when the M3 motorway was being built with its henge-destroying disregard for history, and I feel even more urgency now, as it appears no sacred site is safe.

Cumhacht na Teanga – Or Why I Keep Trying to Learn Irish

Cumhacht na teanga means 'the power of language' in Irish Gaelic, a language I have been trying since my teens to learn. I have a limited proficiency reading it at this point and some ability to converse in writing; my accent when speaking is probably horrifying. So why, after almost 20 years, do I keep trying, keep working at it, when it's obviously such a challenge?

I have many reasons, of course, for people who ask. First and foremost is that I *want* to speak it, fluently, and I am driven by the desire to teach my children to speak it. It's the language of my ancestors and makes me feel connected to them and to the Gods I honor (as a side note of ancestral languages I also speak German, in which I was at one point fluent). I am also keenly aware of how few people still speak Irish and how easily it could go the way of Cornish and Manx, declared 'dead' languages and now seeing efforts at revival. It pains me to think of Irish as a dead language, with all its beauty and lyricism reduced to history books and old songs.

Second of all it would make studying the material I study easier. In much of the scholarly writings and folklore Gaelic words are used to convey concepts or descriptions and I want to know what those words mean, not just guess from context. I also have many dual language editions of myths and I want to know how similar they are to the translations. I want to be able to read the material directly and draw my own conclusions, instead of relying on someone else's opinions.

Another driving reason is that I want to understand the culture of the Irish, and so much of culture is conveyed in language, or perhaps we could say that language is an inherent expression of culture. It shapes how we think and how we relate to the world and other people; language in many ways is a direct reflection of culture. In psychology we call this the Whorf-Sapir hypothesis. Although this hypothesis is not supported by everyone, I do believe that language shapes how we relate to the world and our culture because it is the main tool of expressing that culture and perception. Idioms are a great example of this, a way that a culture expresses unique ideas through language.

In CR and neopagan Druidism there is a continuous discussion about the need to learn a Celtic language. Many persuasive arguments are put forth over the value of language and of the need for those following Celtic paths to honor that path by learning the language of the culture they study. For me all of that is moot; I am driven to learn Irish by an intrinsic force, the same kind that makes me write poetry or calls me to be a polytheist. I feel as if the language is a part of who I am in some way, no matter how poorly I speak it now, and no matter how long it takes I will keep trying.

Tir gan teanga, tir gan anam.

Sacred Tattooing

I have always seen tattooing as a sacred process, a way to permanently embed images and symbols into the flesh that have a transcendent meaning. All of my tattoos contain this level of meaning and are first and foremost for me spiritual and secondarily artwork. Even the process of being tattooed has spiritual implications for me, and I have often approached the experience as an offering to the Gods and spirits. There is, so far, no concrete evidence of the Celtic peoples using tattooing but there is evidence of tattooing in similar cultures, including the Picts, which made me want to explore the concept of tattooing in the ancient world, specifically in Europe.

The earliest know tattoo work found was on the so-called Ice Man, a preserved body found in the area between Italy and Austria. This body was dated to 3000 BCE, making it over 5,000 years old (Lineberry, 2007). The body displayed tattooed patterns on the lower back, knee, and ankle which led researchers to conclude the tattoos were mostly therapeutic in nature, being placed on areas with signs of degeneration (Lineberry, 2007). From this it would seem that the earliest tattoos could have been used in a medicinal fashion, although exactly how can only be guessed at.

Additionally tattooing was believed to have been used among the Scythians and Picts. Several preserved Scythian bodies have been found dating as far back as 2400 BCE and both the male and female bore tattoos, in some cases very elaborate, depicting animals and mythic images (Lineberry, 2007). In his writings Herodotus remarked that among the Scythians, 'tattoos were a mark of nobility, and not to have them was testimony of low birth.' This could indicate that by the time Herodotus was writing – around 450 BCE – tattooing had become a sign of social standing. The stylized images seen in the Scythian tattoos are the same as those seen in other Scythian artwork, indicating that the tattoos reflected larger social concepts and symbolism (Kromarik, 2003). In the case of the Picts less is known with certainty because no preserved bodies have been found. Writings from secondary sources indicate that Pictish tattoos, like the Scythian, were a symbol of status and that they included images of animals (Lineberry, 2007). Herodian, writing around 200 CE says that the Celts, 'draw figures of animals or symbols on their skin by pressing hot iron onto their limbs, causing great pain, and over this they rub the sap of a plant.' (Green, 2012). While this account is questionable because the writer never traveled to any of the Celtic lands and was likely repeating another person's experience, there are other Roman sources that mention the use of iron implements to create permanent marks, which means it was either a widespread belief by the Romans or may have been the actual practice. As late as 600 CE a Christian bishop noted the practice of tattooing among the Picts, mentioning a process similar to that cited by Herodian, except pricking was used in place of hot iron (Green, 2012).

Other cultures that used tattoos included the Egyptians, Nubians, and some areas of the Americas. Tattooing would later spread to the Greeks and Romans, initially as a way to mark a person as being dedicated to a temple or as a slave (Lineberry, 2007). However, the advent of Christianity slowly discouraged the practice of tattooing, which was seen as defiling the body, although it is seeing a modern resurgence.

The true meaning behind ancient tattoos in many of these cultures will never be known, but we do know that tattooing was a common practice among some ancient cultures. The evidence also supports the theory that these tattoos, particularly among the Picts and Scythians, were more than mere decoration. Whether the Irish Celts tattooed or not we may never know. I am comfortable with my own view of the sacredness of tattooing and will undoubtedly continue to add spiritually meaningful tattoos to my own body.

References:

Lineberry, C., (2007). Tattoos. Retrieved from http://www.smithsonianmag.com/history-archaeology/tattoo.html

Kromarik, K., (2003). History of Tattooing. Retrieved from https://www.msu.edu/~krcmari1/individual/history.html

Green, T., (2012). Ancient Celtic Tattooing. Retrieved from http://www.tattoosymbol.com/celtic/ancient_celtic.html

Conclusion

Living Druidism

Do réir a chéile a tógtar na caisleáin.

I've been thinking a lot lately about what it means to me to be a Druid, a title that for me represents a bridge between the ancient and the new. How does it shape my life? How does it affect me?

This may seem like a simple question, but I've struggled to grasp it now for a while. It's like asking how does being a woman shape my life; it influences so many aspects of my being that it is, in its own way, an intrinsic part of who I am. I tend to favor seeing the word Druid as a title, but in some vital ways it has ceased to have that meaning for me – or rather has gone beyond that – and become part of who I am. I am a Druid. If I never held another ritual, if I never taught another class, if I never sought imbas, if I ceased every action that defines the word Druid for me, I would still be a Druid because the external actions have become only a reflection of the inner process. I do not know when this happened, or how, but I know it is true.

So, how do I feel that my life reflects my religious path and role? I feel a driving responsibility to help those that need help. I teach. I run rituals for the public when I can. I care for the world I live in so that it will continue to be able to support all of us by recycling and living as best I can with nature. I try to be knowledgeable so that I can answer questions when people need answers. I hone my skills, be they magical or mundane, so that I can use them when they are needed. I do my best to serve my community when and how I can. I pass on what I know to my children and my students. I strive, not to live in harmony, but to nurture that which creates the best outcome for myself, my family, and my community. I actively use what I know and what

I can do, magically, when I think it needs to be used. I pray to the Gods and spirits, make offerings, and do everything I can to nurture a strong relationship with them. But do my actions make me a Druid?

Being a Druid is judged by others based on external actions; either I fit that individual's perception of what a Druid is or I don't. My actions are judged as if they were my beliefs, yet they are only a reflection of my beliefs. I do not live an honorable life because it is what's expected or to fulfill a standard, I live an honorable life because I know that is the best way to live. I know that everything has a spirit and so I honor those spirits. I know the beauty and fierceness, power and vastness of the Gods, and so I honor them in word and deed. I know that my ancestors are with me still and so I talk to them and include them in my life. I know the might and mystery of the daoine sidhe and so I respect them. I know that energy is endless and so I have learned how to understand magic as a tool and use it when I need it. I know that all things are connected and how to read those connections under certain circumstances. I know the paths and ways of the Otherworld. I can read the sky where I live, and understand the trees and plants. I know that great wisdom lives in the old stories and folktales, myths and legends. I listen and hear the song of the aos sidhe, look and see the flow of energy, feel the potential of life. I know these things in my heart and my mind, and I live them in my spirit; my actions are a reflection of this knowing. That is what makes me a Druid.

There was a point in my life when I acted like I thought a Druid should act because I thought that was what made someone a Druid. I understand now that acting like a Druid and being a Druid are wholly different things. One is based only on action. The other is rooted in the soul.

Recommended Reading Lists

I'm limiting it to ten each to keep myself from going totally overboard, but have tried to choose a top-ten recommended reading list for the areas this book covers:

Irish Reconstruction Reading List

1) The CR FAQs. The best basic start to understanding reconstruction from a Celtic viewpoint.
2) the Sacred Isle by D. O'hOgain - discusses Irish religion from pre-Christian times through conversion.
3) Festival of Lughnasa by M. MacNeill. An in-depth look at the historic and modern celebration of Lughnasa, including a good deal of folklore and mythology.
4) The Lebor Gabála Érenn. The story of the invasions of Ireland by the Gods and spirits and eventually humans.
5) Cath Maige Tuired. The story of the battle of the Tuatha de Danann with the Fomorians.
6) The Year in Ireland by K. Danaher. An overview of holidays and folk practices throughout the year.
7) The Silver Bough (all four volumes) by F. McNeill. Scottish but extremely useful for understanding folk practices and belief.
8) Fairy and Folktales of the Irish Peasantry by W. B. Yeats. A look at folklore and belief.
9) Lady with a Mead Cup by M. J. Enright. Useful look at ritual structure and society in both Celtic and Norse cultures.
10) Celtic Gods and Heroes by Sjoestedt.Discusses both the Gods and tidbits of folklore and mythology.

Druid Reading List

1) The Druid's Primer by Luke Eastwood. A good basic introduction to Druidism.

2) Mysteries of Druidry by Brendan Myers. A very useful book exploring modern Irish Druidism.
3) Blood and Mistletoe by Professor Ronald Hutton. A look at the historic Druids as well as the Druid revival.
4) Exploring the World of the Druids by Miranda Green. A good basic look at the ancient Celts and the Druids.
5) A Druid's Herbal by Ellen Evert Hopman. Full of useful information.
6) Bonewits's Essential Guide to Druidism by Isaac Bonewits. An overview of the modern Druid movement and its main branches.
7) The Apple Branch by Alexei Kondratiev. A basic view of Celtic holidays and ritual ideas.
8) Celtic Flame by Aedh Rua. Not Druidic specific but useful for a modern Druid looking at ideas on how to structure practice along more reconstructionist lines.
9) Celtic Seers' Sourcebook by John Matthews. Essential for understanding the practices of Celtic seership.
10) Druid Sourcebook by John Matthews. A great resource for historic sources on Druidism.

Fairy Reading List

1) Fairies: Real Encounters with Little People by Janet Bord. A collection of stories of encounters different people have had with fairies.
2) The Gaelic Otherworld by J. G. Campbell. Classic Scottish collection of fairy folklore
3) The Fairy Faith in Celtic Countries by W. Y. Evans Wentz. The classic text on the Fairy Faith, a must read for anyone interested in the subject.
4) Scottish Herbs and Fairy Lore by Ellen Evert Hopman. A fascinating look at different aspects of Scottish fairy lore and practice.
5) Faeries by Brian Froud and Alan Lee (most anything by

Froud has value). Worth getting just for the artwork, although it also contains a wealth of folklore.

6) Elves, Wights and Trolls by Kveldulf Gundarsson. A fascinating comparison of Norse and Irish fairy beliefs; primarily focused on the Norse material.
7) The Secret Commonwealth of Elves, Fauns and Fairies by Robert Reverend Kirk. One of the oldest written texts on fairies, this work provides good insight into the older beliefs.
8) Meeting the Other Crowd: The Fairy Stories of Hidden Ireland by E. Lenihan and C. E. Green. This book is another extremely useful collection of anecdotal evidence.
9) The Elemental Encyclopedia of Magical Creatures by John and Caitlin Matthews. An encyclopedia style book that lists many common types of fairies.
10) Celtic Twilight by William Butler Yeats. A collection of poetry and essays about Irish fairy lore. My personal favorite.

I have also heard that Brian Walsh's book The Secret Commonwealth and the Fairy Belief Complex is very good, but I haven't had a chance to read it yet.

Heathen Reading List

1) Essential Asatru by Diana Paxson. A good introduction to the basics of belief and practice, particularly useful for those coming from a neopagan background.
2) The Prose Edda. I suggest reading multiple translations to get the best understanding of the material.
3) The Poetic Edda. Multiple translations are your friend.
4) The Norse Myths by Kevin Crossley-Holland. Modern language retellings of the Eddic myths.
5) The Road to Hel by H.R. Ellis Davidson. An essential look at beliefs about the dead and afterlife.

6) The Well and the Tree by Paul Bauschatz. Discusses cosmology from a heathen perspective.
7) Our Troth, volumes 1 and 2 by Kveldulf Gundarsson. A very thorough look at everything from belief to practice, and a wonderful reference to have on hand.
8) Elves, Wights, and Trolls by Kveldulf Gundarsson. A look at the heathen belief in Otherworldly spirits, often not emphasized in American heathenry but very important to understand.
9) Living Asatru by Greg Shelter. Short but useful look at living modern asatru.
10) We Are Our Deeds by Eric Wodening. A very in depth look at modern heathen ethics

Bibliography

Anderson, G., (2008). Birds of Ireland: Facts, Folklore and History. Collins Press

Berresford Ellis, P., (1987). Dictionary of Irish Mythology. Oxford University Press

Bitel, L., (1996). Land of Women. Cornell University Press

Carmichael, A., (1900). Carmina Gadelica volume 1. Retrieved from http://www.sacred-texts.com/neu/celt/cg1/cg1057.htm

Culpeper, N., Culpeper's Complete Herbal (1649 reprinted 2007). Sterling

Da Silva, B., (2009). Saint Patrick, the Irish Druids, and the Conversion of Pagan Ireland to Christianity. Retrieved from http://www.strangehorizons.com/2009/20090727/da_silva-a.shtml

Daimler, M., (2010). By Land, Sea, and Sky. Lulu Publishing

Danaher, K., (1972). The Year in Ireland. The Mercier Press

Estyn Evans, E., (1957). Irish Folk Ways. Dover Publications

Evans, D., (2011). Nudd. Retrieved from http://www.celtnet.org.uk/Gods_n/nudd.html

Evans Wentz, W., (1911). The Fairy Faith in Celtic Countries http://www.sacred-texts.com/neu/celt/ffcc/ffcc310.htm

Evert Hopman, E. (1995). A Druid's Herbal for the Sacred Earth Year. Destiny Books

Fraser Black, G., (1894). Scottish Charms and Amulets. Kessinger Publishing

Freeman, P., (2002). War, Women, and Druids. University of Texas Press

Green, M., (1992). Dictionary of Celtic Myth and Legend. Thames and Hudson

Green, T., (2012). Ancient Celtic Tattooing. Retrieved from http://www.tattoosymbol.com/celtic/ancient_celtic.html

Grieve, M., (1971). A Modern Herbal. Dover

Gwynn E., (1906), The Metrical Dindshenchas. Royal Irish Academy

Gray, E., (1983). Cath Maige Tuired. Irish Texts Society

Irish Fireside (2011). All About That Celtic hair. http://irish-fireside.com/2011/08/25/all-about-that-celtic-hair/

Jones, M., (2012). Nodens http://www.maryjones.us/jce/nodens.html

Joyce, P., (1908). A Smaller Social History of Ancient Ireland. Retrieved from http://www.alia.ie/tirnanog/sochis/sochis01.html#iv

Keating, G., (1857). Foras Feasa ar Éirinn. Ulan Press

Kellnhauser, J. (1993). The Excellence of Ancient Word: Druid Rhetorics from Ancient Irish Tales. Retrieved from http://www.imbas.org/articles/excellence_of_the_ancient_word.html

Kelly, F., (1988). A Guide to Early Irish Law. Dublin Institute for Advanced Studies

Kondratiev, A., (1998). The Apple Branch: A Path to Celtic Ritual. Citadel

Kromarik, K., (2003). History of Tattooing. Retrieved from https://www.msu.edu/~krcmari1/individual/history.html

Leabhar na h-Uidre (nd) Retrieved from http://www.maryjones.us/ctexts/flidais.html

Leahy, A., (1906). Heroic Romances of Ireland. Tradition

Lineberry, C., (2007). Tattoos. Retrieved from http://www.smithsonianmag.com/history-archaeology/tattoo.html

MacAlister. R. (1941). Lebor Gabála Érenn. Irish Texts Society

MacKillop, J., (1998). A Dictionary of Celtic Mythology. Oxford University Press

MacNeill, M., (1962). The Festival of Lughnasa. Folklore of Ireland Council

Markale, J., (1986). Women of the Celts. Inner Traditions

Martin, M., (1695). A Description of the Western Isles. Birlinn Ltd.

Matthews, J., (1998). The Druid Sourcebook. Sterling Publishing co.

Matthews, J., (1999). Celtic Seers' Sourcebook. Cassell Illustrated

McNeill, F. (1959). The Silver Bough volume 1. William MacLellan

McNeill, F., (1959). The Silver bough volume 2. William MacLellan

McNeill, F., (1961). The Silver Bough, volume 3. William MacLellan

Meyers, K., (1906). The Triads of Ireland. Retrieved from http://www.ucc.ie/celt/online/T103006.html

Monaghan, P., (2004). Encyclopedia of Celtic Mythology and Folklore. Checkmark Books

Nodens (2012). Websters Online Dictionary. http://www.websters-online-dictionary.org/definitions/Nodens

O'Dubhain, S., (1999). Druidic Clothing and Dress. Retrieved October 4, 2010 from http://www.summerlands.com/crossroads/library/druidic_clothing%20_and_dress.htm

O hÓgain, D., (1995). Irish Superstitions. Gill & MacMillan

O hÓgain, D., (2006). The Lore of Ireland. Boydell Press

O hÓgain, D., (1999). The Sacred Isle. The Boydell Press

O Suilleabhain, S., (1967). Nosanna agus Piseoga ne nGeal. Cultural Relations Committee of Ireland

Rolleston, T., (n.d.). Myths and Legends of the Celtic Race. Retrieved from http://www.sacred-texts.com/neu/celt/mlcr/mlcr05.htm

Saint Patrick (n.d.). Saint Patrick's Confessio http://www.cin.org/patrick.html

Sjoestedt, M., (1949). Celtic Gods and Heroes. Dover Publications

Stokes, W., (1898), O'Mulconry's Glossary

Troth (2006). Our Troth volume 1. Book Surge Publishing

Viking Answer Lady (2012). Courtship, Love and Marriage in Viking Scandinavia and Viking Age Hairstyles, Haircare and Personal Grooming. Retrieved http://www.vikinganswerlady.com/wedding.shtml and http://www.vikinganswerlady.com/hairstyl.shtml

Wilde, (1991). Irish Cures, Mystic Charms & Superstitions. Sterling.

Endnotes

1 Invoke, despite modern pagan misconceptions of the word, means:

1. *To call on (a higher power) for assistance, support, or inspiration*

2. *To appeal to or cite in support or justification.*

3. *To call for earnestly; solicit (http://www.thefreedictionary.com/invoke)*

I use words based on definition not popular perception or urban legend style meanings.

2 More on Nodens – also known in Wales as Nudd, or Llud Llaw Eirent (Llud the silver handed), sometimes equated to the Irish Nuada, and on the continent as Noadatus. Possibly a pan-Celtic deity synchronized with Mars, sometimes Silvanus, and in one case Neptune; his name may mean 'Water Maker' or 'Spirit of Water', although it is equally likely to mean 'He who Catches' (Evans, 2011; Jones, 2012). A God of healing who had a shrine in Gloucestershire where votive offerings were made of bronze objects representing the area of the body the person needed to be healed, particularly limbs and eyes (Green, 1992). He is especially associated with amputees because he was believed to have lost an arm in battle, which was later replaced with a silver one, hence the epithet 'silver hand'. His companion is a dog who can heal wounds by licking them; besides dogs, he is particularly associated with salmon and trout which may make good offerings to him (Evans, 2011).

3 Worship means ardent devotion or adoration, from the middle English 'worshipe' which meant worthiness, honor. I have no issue using this word to describe what I do in honoring my ancestors, but some people feel strongly about not using this word, and prefer to use veneration, or honor.

My use of the word worship is a choice, but I understand others may choose differently; if the word usage bothers you feel free to replace it with 'veneration', a synonym for worship that may be more acceptable.

4 If anyone is curious about why I place the ceremony with the ritual fire on the second day and not on the first where it should more logically be – the first night is very much about doing as much as I can with my children and my youngest daughter, at this point, has several issues that make anything involving total darkness a bad idea. I am still working out what exactly should go where, ritually speaking, and next year I hope to have the fire on the first night in a more 'traditional' way since fire was such a major part of this holiday. But in the year of writing this book, this is how things worked out. Sometimes you just have to roll with it.

5 Based on a prayer from page 123 of volume 1 of the Carmina Gadelica. The original is:
If to-night, O moon, thou hast found us
In peaceful, happy rest
May thy laving oliag leave us
Seven times still more blest.
O moon so fair,
May it be so,
As seasons come,
And seasons go.
It can be found at http://sacred-texts.com/neu/celt/cg1/cg1057.htm

6 Modified from a prayer out of volume 1 of the Carmina Gadelica

7 Modified from a prayer out of volume 1 of the Carmina Gadelica

8 Imbas is an Old Irish word that means inspiration or knowledge

9 From the eDIL:

fáidetóracht
ā,f. prophesying, prophecy; second sight: do firadh an faidhedóracht sin BCC § 104 dorinde se faidhetoracht don baile sin § 207 . an fháidhedóracht § 66 . tre spiraid fhaidhedorachta § 352 . go ffuil spirat fhaid- etorachta innam, Fl. Earls 222 although often given heavy Biblical connotations.
Fáitsine may be another option, although it may be that Fili really is the best word and I'm just making this harder for myself because the modern connotation is so strongly poetic and not as much emphasis on prophecy or divination.

10 Most modern seidhr workers that I know of use a veil to cover the face during oracular work. I use a bear skin, with the face covering my own, because that's how I was told to do it. I don't argue with the people who have my back. By a wyrd coincidence the bear was given to me by a family member shortly after I was told I needed one, after it had spent many years as a rug; since acquiring it I made some offerings to its spirit so that we are all copacetic.

11 From the Carmina Gadelica: 'The 'frith' of the Celt is akin to the 'frett' of the Norseman. Probably the surnames Freer, Frere, are modifications of 'frithir,' augurer.'

12 McNeill does reference 'clach nathrach' (serpent stone), also called a Druidical bead said to be created in the same way, by snakes, but found in Scotland on the ground, possibly referring to a common type of stone of an unknown (to me) type. This stone was used to protect against enchantments, for healing, and for childbirth.

Moon Books invites you to begin or deepen your encounter with Paganism, in all its rich, creative, flourishing forms